D1002624

Knowledge is Power...

When Life Gives You Children

IZZY REHAUME

Published by
Union Square Publishing
New York, NY 10022
www.unionsquarepublishing.com

Copyright © 2017 by Izzy Rehaume

All rights reserved. No part of this book may be reproduced or transmitted in any form or by in any means, electronic or mechanical, including photocopying, recording, or by any information storage and retrieval system, without the written permission of the Publisher, except where permitted by law.

Manufactured in the United States of America, or in the United Kingdom when distributed elsewhere.

Rehaume, Izzy
    When Life Gives You Children: Knowledge is Power
    LCCN: 2017952723
    ISBN: 978-1-946928-08-5
    eBook: 978-1-946928-09-2

Cover design by: Julie Rehaume
Cover illustration by: Bryan Ubaghs
Interior design by: Claudia Volkman
Book illustrations by: Athena T. Thomas
Edited by: Angela Black

www.whenlifegivesyouchildren.com/

DEDICATION

This Look Before You Leap book is dedicated to the pre-parent, new parent, single parent, or those who are thinking about becoming parents, on this, or any other planet overrun by their offspring.

"There are only two lasting bequests we can hope to give our children. One of these is roots, the other, wings."

JOHANN WOLFGANG VON GOETHE

TABLE OF CONTENTS

"Before I got married I had six theories about bringing up children; now I have six children and no theories."

JOHN WILMOT

PRE-RAMBLE

There have been many books written by authors who claim to be experts on the subject of raising kids. While thousands of doctors, therapists and other specialists have dedicated thousands of hours in researching new ways to raise children—and often *do* present some good advice—they can fall short at times because their recommendations are usually geared for *after* you have children *(which means it's too late).*

What sometimes isn't explained enough is how the standard day-to-day life of parenting can be too much for any analytical thought or reason to occur. In other words, no matter how well-intended the experts are, their advice can become nothing more than a blur of afterthoughts left to swirl down the bathtub drain along with the car oil, kitty litter, and dog food.

To illustrate this even further, picture if you will five or six bloodthirsty Tasmanian (dare)devils, all screaming at the top of their lungs, rampantly weaving trails of mud throughout your pitiful excuse of a home, while, at the same time, you're on the phone with a bill collector and entertaining guests—who *also* have umpteen screaming kids! This is also not to mention being ambushed, hog-tied, and interrogated by said (dare)devils every time you try to use the only bathroom in the house because *your* bladder's blaring! Attempting an authoritative bribe like, "You can have ice cream if you behave…" Or a loving, but firm, "No, no… Stop shaving the cat's head…" Just doesn't work. After years of relentless minute-by-minute, day-in-and-day-out, nonstop power struggles, it's more like, "OH DEAR LORD HELP ME! PLEEEASE HELP ME!! WHAT HAVE I DONE?!!"

That being said, you also have to keep in mind, kids are people too. They have their good days and bad days just like the rest of us. As an example, parents are expected to treat their children with respect, right? After all, kids' glands are still developing, which can cause them to be overactive and have short attention spans. They learn about personal interactions while their little bodies grow into bigger bodies. They also build their own cute little facades and social filters, just like the rest of us, right? Well, this is all fine and dandy–in theory. However, no matter which psychobabble you buy, the bottom line is this: when it comes to parenting, your life does a complete flip before spinning completely out of control at the speed of light toward a galaxy manifesting six time streams to your left!

It is for this reason, I was inspired to write this "LOOK BEFORE YOU LEAP!" book so that maybe–just maybe–I could help the pre-parent REALISTICALLY understand what parenting is all about–*before* deciding to spawn!

"Now the thing about having a baby—and I can't be the first person to have noticed this— is that thereafter you have it."

JEAN KERR

INTRODUCTION

Can you say, "INSANE?!" I too was an "expert" at raising kids—*before* I had them. I would watch other parents lose their cool at the grocery store and say to myself, "Boy, I would never treat my kids that way." Yeah, well... Other than learning a few dos and don'ts *(mostly don'ts)* along the way, I quickly discovered just how far from being an "expert" I truly was.

In this day and age, there are many types of parents. They come in all sorts of ages, shapes, and sizes—old ones, tall ones, skinny ones, and rich ones too! However, all parents have one thing in common—RESPONSIBILITY!

As a parent, you are thrown onto a never-ending, vacillating mental treadmill of obligation, dedication, and complete devotion. From the initial lusty howl of your very first newborn, your aura transforms. You will valiantly don the parenthood mantle, trumpeting out, *"Behold, I Am Parent: Responsible, Accountable, Reliable, and Faster than a Speeding Bullet!"*

Make no mistake about it! Your newborn's arrival is a cunning infiltration and acquisition of your complete mind, body, and spirit! As with all newborns around the world, it starts out with their helpless and beguiling cries, as they lay so innocently in their new little cribs, and ends with all of their parent's undying and fixated attention wrapped around their every whim! Parents don't see it happen right away, but their firstborn slowly and methodically clears the way for the arrival of the younger siblings (i.e., his or her army of lieutenants).

After several years of introspection and wondering what the heck happened, it finally dawns on you—this process is simply your child's way of forging and shaping you into becoming his or her *Sword and Shield*. In other words, kids need a challenging yet safe environment from which to learn, and like most parents, you'll eagerly agree to their plans. After all, who could say "no" to such cute little bundles of joy?

As *Sword and Shield*, you become *Protector*, *Defender*, *Provider*, *Loyal Subject*, *Patsy*, and *Mule*. You name it, that's you! Your children become the whimsical hands, pulling and tugging at your strings as you stumble, frolic, and dance around them like their personal marionette!

Throughout each day, your puppeteers (*a.k.a. your children*) test the strength, honor, courage, and devotion that their new puppet can provide. From challenging their teachers at school, to antagonizing the cashiers at the store, to even pitting you against yourself, they'll forge, and shape, and forge, and shape their hand-crafted, *Sword and Shield*.

After years of this coercive persuasion, you will become as malleable and suggestible as a newborn baby puppy. The only difference is that this molding and shaping also comes with a reinforced, laser-precision, *blind obedience* trigger. You'll do anything to protect and defend this little army—even if it drains every last breath of life out of you.

And, as thousands of parents before you, you'll find yourself charging head-on through that never-ending and ever-growing battlefield of commitment, obligation, and patience. Yeah, good old patience: *The bearing of provocation, annoyance, and pain without complaint or irritation or loss of temper...* Yup, patience: The painstaking ability to endure–FOR LIFE–the effects caused by your children.

Before I had kids of my own, the word "patience" didn't mean much to me at all. I was minding my own business and living *my* life, free as a bird, and choosing my battles wisely. However, after the little monst... I mean children, came along, I learned the word "patience" did in fact have meaning; but, along with a lot of my hair, I seemed to have lost it somewhere. I was no longer able to choose my battles. I was catapulted into the front lines of my children's lives–forever.

Unless you have the attributes of a perfect and flawless human being, you might as well check yourself into the nearest *Loony Lollipop Factory!* Even if you consider yourself to be an "atheist" and have never prayed before, *this will be the time when you start.* In fact, you'll be praying all the time. At first, you quietly pray to yourself; and then, as the years go by, your prayers crescendo into an emphatic imploring, *"God save me! Oh God, please save me!"*

Eventually, you have no choice but to become a completely deranged, sleep-deprived, over-caffeinated, bug-eyed parent, sitting on the floor in your favorite corner babbling incoherently and playing *Twiddly-Lips* with your fingers! Ah, yes. Your little corner. Your chapel of solace. You will come to know it very well.

Actually, it's not as bad as it sounds. It's WORSE! Much worse!

When your second child is born, you're not just a parent anymore. Nope. You've just been assigned a new position: *Referee!* Yup! That's right. And with two or more kids, you've just been estab-

lished as the lifelong referee in a game of, *Kill the Ref!*

When you become a parent, you will find you also write off many things. You'll naturally trade in your personal plans, projects, and goals—as well as all of your money, sleep, and time—for soggy, poop-filled diapers! Most of all, parenting leads to the loss of the only thing you really started out with: YOUR MIND! And don't even try to remember what sex was. That's out. Besides, sex is what got you to trade in your sanity for parenthood in the first place. There's an old and wise saying, "He who plays with..." ah, never mind. If you're already a parent, it's probably too late for that.

Ah, yes, those sweet and innocent little creatures our grandparents and elderly strangers sometimes refer to as "little angels" possess the ability to smash, level, devastate, ravage, demolish, rip, annihilate, extinguish, and ultimately destroy the once sound and healthy minds of their parents. Our kids, what would we ever do without them?

If you want mind-boggling, spine-tingling, nail-biting, anxiety-filled, cliff-hanging thrills by the minute, that's what you get *When Life Gives You Children!* This pandemonium of screams, whistles, and water bills will suck every gasp of life out of you with such a high rate of velocity, you'll have no doubt you've been thrown down the greatest rabbit hole of them all!

So welcome to parenthood! *And may God have mercy on your soul!*

(Special Note: While this book is not intended to be a biography, all of the experiences shared are true to the author, but the names have been changed to protect the guilty.)

"Look before you leap for as you sow, ye are like to reap."

SAMUEL BUTLER

"Familiarity breeds contempt
—and children."

MARK TWAIN

PREGNANCY & BIRTH

The hostile takeo... Er, I mean, child rearing usually begins several months prior to the actual birth. And, in most cases, becoming a parent means *both parents* become pregnant—which leads to each parent developing their own perspective of what their particular roles are in being a parent.

The Father's Perspective...

From pregnancy on, the expectant mother uses this time to simply lay around the house relaxing her days into a tranquil bliss, while the expectant father, without a second thought, devotes and caters all of his selfless love, care, and undivided attention to his mate's every whim and need.

Prior to going to work each day (digging ditches with his bare hands in the sub-zero degree, dead-of-icy-freezing-cold-winter weather), the expectant father will fluff his true love's pillows, rub her tired, aching feet, and give her a full body massage with the warm body oils that he has so thoughtfully heated up an hour earlier on the fire he quietly built in the fireplace. He'll also make sure

everything she needs is only a fingertip away; such as the remote for the TV, her favorite reading materials, beloved ice cream bars, and a hot pot of tea (ready for her to pour throughout the rest of the morning while he is away).

While the father-to-be is at work, he will risk his job and life by sneaking away on company time to call home every hour ensuring that his beloved sweetheart is safe and sound. And, during his lunch breaks, he rushes home to prepare and serve her favorite brunch of freshly cut relishes and a bowl of steaming hot soup to keep her snuggled and warm.

After a quick *(yet soothing)* foot massage while humming his precious angel a gentle lullaby to ease her back into her peaceful slumber, he tenderly kisses her forehead and quietly makes his exit. Blowing his warm and happy home a kiss, he then pushes his car down the cold and icy street before jumping in and starting it, so as not to disturb or startle her... Off to his slavish, never-ending, dead-end job he goes.

He arrives home from work every night with a different bouquet of flowers and a new poem he's written especially for her. He immediately and graciously prepares and serves her a romantic, candle-lit dinner complete with freshly squeezed, sparkling fruit juices, as romantic melodies quietly flow from the stereo.

To conclude their evenings, the expectant father then pours his dreamboat a warm bubble-bath and slowly massages hot oils onto her vulnerable, soft shoulders... Preparing himself for the standard midnight runs to the store for the ingredients to make her favorite artichoke & peanut butter ice cream sandwiches. Ah, marital bliss.

The Mother's Perspective...

To the father's complete *(yet understanding)* astonishment, mom's recollection of this time period is blurred with vague delusions of her having to slave over a hot oven all day while at the same time scrubbing and cleaning the walls, floors, and ceilings with her bare fingernails and teeth... Not to mention catering to the expectant father and all his drinking buddies as they simply lay around on the couch watching football and drinking beer all day...

Fortunately, these hallucinations can easily be dismissed as symptoms of, "Postpartum Depression." Unfortunately, and to the father's utter dismay, there is no cure for this lifelong illness.

The Pregnancy...

Sometime during the eighth month of pregnancy the mother-to-be all of a sudden realizes she's going to have a baby. As a result, she decides it's time to make way for the long-awaited arrival. This is called "the nesting period." Along with cleaning and scrubbing the walls and floors behind every single refrigerator, oven, and entertainment center within arm's reach, as well as spit-shining the toilet brush, the mother-to-be uses this time to pick themes and colors for the new nursery. She will spend hours upon hours negotiating between 60 trillion samples of window treatments, blankets, mobiles, and paint swatches—but not before she's thoroughly rearranged and remodeled the garage first. Not to worry though, after the first child is born, "nesting" *never happens again*.

Next, you have Lamaze classes to attend. Upon your arrival, you can't help but notice the instructor frantically running around hiding all of the sharp objects in the room as all the pregnant couples enter. Along with learning different *Tic-Tac-Toe* strategies on the mother-to-be's stretch marks, Lamaze teaches "breath control."

Breath control, once mastered, means the birthing room "fills with distant sounds of ocean waves crashing against the shores..." As the mother-to-be calmly breathes and delivers her newborn infant into the harmonious and soothing comforts of this "glorious and peaceful" world. (The only actual sound of "distant ocean waves" that takes place is the waving of a clipboard over the expectant father's unconscious head after it has bounced three times across the bed frame to finally lay to rest on to the freezing cold delivery room linoleum floor.)

In order to monitor the pregnancy for preparation of the baby's long-awaited arrival, there are many trips to the doctor. This also means the drive to the hospital will be imbedded forever in your memory from the 3,694 "false alarms" you'll be put through for the two-and-a-half weeks just prior to *(each and every)* delivery. If you notice you're grinding the gears *(even though you're driving an automatic)*, as well as mistaking the brakes for the clutch, don't worry. This is perfectly normal. *(If that rodeo ride doesn't put a few centimeters on the ol' cervix, nothin' will!)*

Just prior to the birth there are certain questions for which you'll need answers. So, it may be a good idea to have a checklist ready. You may need to know such things as:

- How many fingers and toes should the kid have?
- Why does the doctor have only nine fingers?
- How many fingers do I have?

- Where are my fingers?!
- What the *#@*?!
- Where am I?!
- Baby?!

There are basically two types of births: *Natural* and *C-section*. As we all know, "C" stands for "cute" and a lot of people opt for having C-sections so they won't have a bunch of little cone-heads running around. From the man's point of view, both procedures are actually a piece of cake and very routine. Regarding "natural birth," mom just spits the kid out on her lunch break and goes back to running her Fortune 500 company, or some such thing. The C-section birth is just about as simple, but the doctor does all the work.

After a succession of screams *(usually from the father)* the newborn finally enters the room amidst an entourage of doctors, nurses, fore-snips, and forceps. Once the kid is out, but not before taking a breath of fresh air, being weighed, and freshened up a bit, he or she is readied for a blurry *(yet memorable)* introduction to his new grandparents, uncles, nieces, cousins... and then, eventually, his parents. And that is that. Yippee!

Let the games begin!

"Pregnancy is a disease
from which you recover in
18 years and 9 months."

CARRIE LATET

"People who say they sleep like a baby usually don't have one."

LEO J. BURKE

2

BEDDY-BYE TIME

Because a parent is on the job 27 hours per day, 12 days per week, let's condense it down somewhat. If dad (or mom) goes to work and is gone from 6:00 in the morning until 6:00 in the evening, Monday through Friday, you may have what would be considered a typical household.

Regarding the newborn who just obliterated your once pleasant, and comparably tranquil dwelling, hold on for dear life! That "little dumpling," lying so innocently in the still unpaid-for crib, is about to rob you of every ounce of sleep you'd ever *dreamed* of having!

Your new schedule will go something like this: If your role is "dad," most of your sleep will occur while you drive to and from work. If your role is "mom"–and if you're *extremely* lucky–you may be able to catch a wink between feedings.

Your sleep will become the main focal point of the day and usually dwindles down to a pathetic, lost cause. This is particularly true if your "little Johnny" has a digestive problem. The loss of sleep alone is enough for you to consider buying that Harley you'd always wanted, and abandon your responsibilities as a parent altogether, by riding off into the sunset–*forever and ever, amen!*

If, eventually, you have multiple children, plus a newborn, you may as well start investing in a padded room at your local wacky bin. Your new game is called, *War!,* and will consist of you trying to defend and protect this new addition to your family from the enemy—your older children.

Part of this game is going to include your feeble attempt at maintaining peace and quiet so no one, for heaven's sake, disturbs the newborn. The older ones quickly learn you can't yell at them because that would help fulfill their objective: to divide and conquer everything—especially YOU! You can't touch them either, as that too would create the disturbance necessary to arouse blood-curdling screams from your now too-awake and too-angry-to-sleep little treasure.

Of course, this is all part of their plot, geared to wrap all of your attention around the whims of the "helpless" infant, so they can then execute their hostile takeover of the house! This usually includes, but is not limited to, building tree forts from the attic to the basement with whatever three-legged chairs, tattered lamp shades, and screwdriver-gouged tables they find still standing. If none of this works, their next objective is to simply kidnap the newborn for ransom.

Going back in time and getting *Attila the Hun* to publicly recant his ways is easier than getting your kids to go right to sleep. You've become a circus trainer, surrounded by roaring tigers, with a whip in one hand, and a chair in the other. Even when you do get them to go to sleep, you need to watch them all very closely, in case one of them does wake up, so he won't wake up the others, as that can be disastrous.

The more kids you have, the more chance there is of kids waking up other kids. This is especially true if one of them becomes ill. Either he will wake up his siblings because he's sick, or they will keep him awake because they are playing—and kids getting ill never fails to happen at 2:30 in the morning. It's an altered state of reality when two of them decide to vomit their way down the hall and into the only chance of a break you so desperately want to call "sleep." Oh well. You weren't really doing anything anyway. Right?

There comes a time when your kids fully understand the last thing you want to do is stand around and supervise them NOT going right to sleep. After all, you certainly have more important things to do, like sit and stare at a TV like a comatose zombie for the rest of your life! However, if their bedrooms are upstairs or downstairs, as the case may be, there are stairs—lots and lots of stairs to contend with.

When you finally give up on running up, down, down, up, up, down, down, up, *ad infinitum*... Your next step is simply to yell at them from the living room couch. How entertaining. This, of course, only escalates their ruckus—once again driving you to run your hamster treadmill: up, down, down, up, down, up, up, down, up, down, etc. They love that: INCOMING DERANGED YELLING PARENT!

When you finally collapse on the couch with your head in your hands from complete and utter exhaustion, the youngest one will come in whimpering, rubbing his head, pointing back to the direction from whence he came. You then scoot him back upstairs and assure him that he'll be "all right."

Five minutes later the oldest one will come into the living room, looking as guilty as can be, to play, *Pass the Blame*. First, he'll tell you, "one of the other" kids threw baby brother off of the bed. And then, as he's flippantly flipping through the pages of a comic book, he'll nonchalantly mention the blood running out of the child's mouth.

The first couple of times this happens, you panic, of course. But, after the SIX-HUNDREDTH *#@*?! TIME a kid enters the room for *ANY* reason, that kid, for all intents and purposes, will be grounded for life! Or worse, made to sit there and listen to your one-hour, "When I was your age…" speech.

To children, the word, "bedtime," never *actually* means it's time to go to sleep. The announcement of bedtime is simply the sound of the "starting gun" to commence ransacking their rooms. This can mean anything from holding mashed potato contests (to see whose clump would stick to the ceiling the longest), to using their toy shovels to catapult the neighbor's cat over the bunk beds, to throwing all of their pillows and blankets out the second story window. In any event, their pillaged rooms and torn-up beds become justification for not going right to sleep. After all, who could sleep in a bed without sheets or blankets?

The older they become, the more excuses they'll create for not going straight to bed. If they're all boys, one of their most favorite games will be, *Target Practice!* In other words, it will be very convenient for them to pee on each other's beds, walls, windows, light fixtures, Legos, and anything else which might happen to be available–including each other.

Target Practice fits nicely into their plans of completely destroying your sanity. They'll set you up every time and wait for the explosion point–your reaction: INCOMING DERANGED YELLING PARENT *(again)*. You finally get to the point where you threaten to rub their noses in it, if it ever happens again. What do they do? Ignore your threat and proceed to pee all over the lower bunk from the upper bunk. What do you do? You follow through with your threat and rub their noses in it. What do they do? Laugh hysterically about it. What do you do? You write a book about it as your last-ditch effort, in the hopes that someone with a lot of money happens to read it and takes pity on you to the point that they…

a) Make a movie and/or a sitcom out of it;
b) Donate a blank check to the author;
c) Hire a hit man to put the poor author out of his misery;
d) All the above.

Other than convincing a younger brother or two to pee on an electric fence, it appeared that baseboard heaters were the next best thing for kids to pee on. The first *(and last)* time it happened in my household, I jolted out of bed to the sirens of a very rude and belligerent smoke alarm blaring in the hallway at 2:00 in the morning. I opened my bedroom door to a violent slap in the face: rising waves of eye-sizzling, vaporizing stench! These noxious fumes made me realize I'd never smelled anything so rank in my life! A family of dead rats having been stuck in a wall for two-and-a-half weeks has the fragrance of a newly blossomed rose compared to the gaseous odors of steaming hot urine.

I jumped into the fray and grabbed the closest weapon available—the broom, standing innocently in the hallway closet—and wildly swung it at the screaming smoke alarm on the ceiling! It simply was THE WORST ODOR IN THE UNIVERSE! If I hadn't known my kids were up to one of their more outrageous escapades, I would have been running around, frantically looking for something resembling a very *dead* Martian! That stuff stank!

Being the clever, yet sleep-deprived, bug-eyed, brain-dead parent that I was, I did stop the baseboard urinating competition from ever happening again by making the guilty parties stay in their "perfume-saturated" room. It was only my concern for their impending brain damage that forced me to finally let them out.

There are hundreds of excuses for kids not going right to sleep, ranging from, "still being thirsty," to, "a death in the family." You can bet if bedtime is at 7:30 p.m., the actual sleeping won't occur until around 10:30 p.m. And quite often, the younger ones will end up in bed with you; and if they are not yet fully potty-trained, you're in for a very dismal night of sleep. Their half-opened baby bottles and overflowing soggy diapers will turn your bed into a marshy, smelly, lactose-intolerant swamp.

Infants will let you know how you can supposedly live without any sleep at all. Night, after night, after night, after night, after night, you find yourself dragging your saggy butt across the house and into the kitchen for the "2 a.m. feeding"–which, by the way, turns into a smorgasbord of juggling bottles, diapers, and your letters of resignation to the parent's union rep–which you find does little good anyway because your petitions always come back marked, "Undelivered," "Return To Sender," or, "On Vacation." In other words:

Eventually, this way of life starts to eat away at every ounce of composure and sense of intelligent reasoning you could possibly muster. And if that's not enough, your little impressionists may even become fascinated at painting their blankets, cribs, walls, and themselves with... Yup, you guessed it–POOP! Ah, the little *Picassos*.

Remember, this does not just happen once or twice. Hour after hour, night after night, this exhaustive process goes on. There are no breaks. None!

There will be "special times" too. Even though you're unfathomably exhausted, you become aware that 1 a.m. to 5 a.m. is their "social hour." Your get-togethers will be quiet and allow for some one-on-one time. When your kids are infants, you might walk them through the house showing them very simple things like how to move the light switches up and down, how to slide the curtains back and forth, or how to open and close the refrigerator. When they become toddlers, you might, as their *Royal Subject/Teacher*, feel compelled to show them a variety of necessary activities such as how to plug in the electrical plugs correctly, how to open and close doors and windows, as well as, how to use the universal remote for the TV, Stereo, DVD, Xbox, Cable, and so on. In my case, it was in the early '80s, before we had all of that, so my kids would learn how to switch the cables in the back of the TV from Cable, to VHS, to Stereo, to Nintendo, etc.

If there will ever be a time when you need patience, this will be it. As *Dr. Professor Parent*, you may think you're educating them to become better prepared for when they become a little older. But remember, this is *War!,* and what you sincerely think is, "bonding time," is actually their "know thy enemy" time.

Staring with rapt attention at the things you are showing them, you assume your kids are very interested and comfortable with learning how this world works. And they *are*. They will study, retain, and adapt to the laws of this universe so they can ultimately use each device you show them to *their* own advantage.

These subtle hints as to who is really in charge can hit you on the head like a cement brick. This became very evident to me when my youngest child was about 18 months old. Still in diapers and armed with his blanket (a royal cape) and his bottle (a royal staff), he would waddle and crawl backward down the stairs to thoroughly survey his kingdom at 2:30 in the morning.

Little did I know how just how well his genius little mind worked. If all was not to "His Royal Liking" in "His Royal Kingdom," he'd simply switch the cables on the TV from VCR to Cable so he could watch his favorite British cult comedy, **Red Dwarf**. I watched him one evening, dumbfounded, and realized he had become *Master Cable Switcher*. In my innocence, what had I done?

Every once in a while, I'd swing through the family room—*Master Cable Switcher's Domain*—to see if "His Royal Highness" needed anything. Scooting over on the couch, he would grant me an audience and summon me to sit. He was always very courteous and hospitable. And, when my appointment was over, he'd give an authoritative royal grunt, point toward the doorway with his bottle/staff and dismiss me. I'd bow and stumble backward out of His Royal Presence and then continue my search for the illusive concept I once knew as sleep. Hear ye, hear he, all was well in his little kingdom.

Nap-time however, is not at all as delightful. It is an altered reality with parallel planes in two different universes—yours and theirs. After having no sleep for 3 years, 14 months, 22 hours and 67 minutes, you might notice you can get very cranky if your li'l banditos don't take their naps. Getting them from a rampant, hyper-kinetic particle acceleration mode to an absolute static inertia (a.k.a. "sleep") is somewhat like unraveling and solving 102.3 different sets of string theories, every day.

First of all, the last thing your children think they need is a nap. No matter how many millions of times you attempt to put them down for their nap, each time will be a brand new experience for them. The thought of taking a nap had simply never entered their thousand-track minds before.

Secondly, because of the, "I'm still thirsty," and the, "I need to go potty," excuses, you will give them all the water they could ever drink and have them go potty until their bladders are completely sterile. If you don't take these two precautions, forget the nap.

And thirdly, just when you think you finally have them "under control," while scooting them two steps from their rooms, they suddenly scatter in every direction for a vigorous game of, *Hide-And-Seek!*

Another dimension added to the universe of nap time is the game, *Let's-Figure-Out-What-the-Problem-Is.* After 15 minutes of the two-year-old screaming and crying, it finally dawns on you—this kid needs a nap!

Your arsenal of warning signs will include the following:

- Constant eye rubbing *(yours as well as the kid's);*
- He wants his milk and juice in one bottle at the same time, but not mixed together;
- He wants his blankets on, but not touching him;

- He wants his lights on and off at the same time;
- 6,000 other indicators, including *your* severe need for a nap—which you're not going to have.

After a while, enough of *What's a Nap?* will excite you to the point of weighing the consequences of death by, A) beating your head in with a peanut butter sandwich or B) jumping out of the basement window. Unfortunately, both alternatives sound good, so the indecision causes you to give up altogether and leave the room at the mercy of your jubilant kids. The next thing you know, you're back in your corner, playing *Twiddly-Lips*, editing your petition for parental resignation, while offering up your daily mantra, *"God save me! Oh God. Please save me!"*

When the house is finally quiet, you might think your alone time has come—*your* time for rest. Ah, the blissful sound of silence. You finally stop the world from turning and can, at long last, float quietly and peacefully into your own world. Right?

Wrong! Now it's time to play, *Entertain the Neighbors!* How do they know your kids are down for a nap? Do they peer through the windows? Do they keep track of your schedule? Or does the noise level dropping by 109 decibels at your house alert them? The neighborhood's quiet. They just know. Along with the Popsicle-man driving up and down your street cranking out 75,000 watts of, *"Yankee Frickin' Doodle Dandy"*—for the umpteenth discordant time, these neighbors' daily visit will play on your very last nerve!

This is the most sacred hour of the day you have for yourself. All you want is to sit in peace and quiet. But, no—this hour is thoroughly consumed by offering your neighbors polite and subtle hints like, "This is the only chance I have to myself, so please leave..." or, "Please leave..." or, "FOR THE LOVE OF ALL THAT IS HOLY! LEAVE ALREADY!!!"

Then, at the first inkling of the pitter-patter of little feet, your neighbors will quickly scatter as though the *Ghost of Christmas Past* had just strolled in. They guzzle down the rest of their coffee and instantly tiptoe backward to the door, gleefully abandoning you with, "Well, it looks like you're going to be busy... so I guess we'll be on our way." How thoughtful!

The number one rule is, of course, **Let A Sleeping Baby Lie!** Never, EVER, wake up a sleeping baby! There may be a time when you might consider repositioning your baby's head after it has hung over a car seat for an hour or two. If you do adjust his head, be very, very certain not to wake him up. What looks comfortable to you may not be for the baby, and you'll end up kicking yourself in the head for being so "thoughtful."

There's almost nothing worse than being on a two-hour car trip with a wet and hungry one-year-old, who has cracked the windshield from screaming four octaves above high C because you accidentally woke him up. The next thing you know, you have one eye on the road, and one hand on the steering wheel, while you're groping through thin air with the other hand trying to capture the screaming, soaking wet, car seat escapee! You become aware that it's time to pull over because the rest of the kids are all now chasing a very upset and bewildered yellow jacket!

To liven things up a bit, this is also when your newly acquired, six-legged, red-haired, greyhound-looking, wannabe-show-dog senses the danger and wants to help out. He decides to leap and frolic and yelp his way from the back of your smoke-billowing 1972 Grand Torino Station Wagon across the rest of the kids to land in your lap in the hopes of taking over the driving altogether.

So be very, very careful about waking up babies. The outcome qualifies for the first Olympic game of, *One Hand/One Eye Driving while Directing a Barnum & Bailey Three Ring Circus!* Not to mention a reckless driving ticket or two.

"Raising kids is part joy
and part guerrilla warfare."

ED ASNER

"Kids don't come with
instructions, they come
with de-structions."

IZZY REHAUME

"I like children — fried."

W. C. FIELDS

3

MEALTIME

Always keep in mind, rambunctious kids usually mean healthy kids. And, healthy kids don't need to know when it's time to eat, because they're eating all the time! Whether it's breakfast, lunch, or dinner, the day will be a blur of one big meal. Mealtime is all the time. The real question is what's available to eat at any given moment?

For instance, with 10-month-old babies, mealtime becomes *Art Time*. The tray on the highchair becomes a palette of colors: spaghetti with peas, carrots, corn, bread, milk, and Jell-O, as well as a launching pad for their ammunition, a.k.a. their food. They will finger paint, face paint, and spray paint everything–the curtains, the ceilings, the floors, the walls, and themselves. With their stockpile of bread-bombs, cache of liquid darts (French fries soaked in milk, juice, and catsup)–and don't forget the bullets of macaroni & cheese–the war is on with the older siblings!

Babies will advance to playing the game of, *Fetch* from their highchair. They throw, you fetch. And, if you don't fetch on command, the screams will boost by 25 decibels. This is an exceptionally fun game for them, because it shows everyone in earshot just how much control they have—and control they *do* have. Simply put, you will be their marionette on strings. They pull, you jump. You'll do just about anything to stop the shrieking demands that siren in all directions from "His Royal Eminence" on "His Royal Throne." Why do you think it's called a "high" chair?

Moving up the food chain... Two-and-a-half-year-olds have an interesting and voracious appetite. Their menu might include such things as, spaghetti mixed with Jell-O cookies, macaroni & cheese à la whip cream, or peanut butter & jelly hot dogs. However, kids can also be interested in more exotic foods such as: beetles, caterpillars, moths, and slugs. Don't be surprised if your five-year-old comes running in screaming, "Joey just put a slug in his mouth!"

As *Great Protector Super Parent*, you drop the laundry right where it stands *(on its own)*, and rush outside to witness your little Joey wandering around the middle of the yard, gurgling half of the slimy slug in his mouth, and the other half in his hand. Ah, a "gourmand" before his time! *"Escargot on a budget,"* you think to yourself. Along with the comedic side to this event, tongue and cheek and all, Joey's surprised face tells you this slug tastes much worse than the caterpillar he ate last week.

Being *Dr. Parent*, it's your duty to get the slug out of his mouth. In your infinite, boundless wisdom, you realize there's only one solution. You hold out the universal garbage can for parents *(your hand)*, and utter the wise words every parent says at least a thousand times a day, "Spit it out!"

Once he heaves up what's left of the slimy slug into your hand, you carry a very willing toddler to the kitchen sink. Without hesitation, he turns up the water to fire-hose capacity and a deluge of water hits his mouth, his face, the ceiling, the curtains, and the walls! Water—the universal solvent and solution.

Curiosity runs high with the other kids. In their world, no one has ever eaten a slug before. They'll want to see what your reaction will be:

- Funny Parent?
- Angry Parent?
- Protector Parent?
- Curious Parent?

You'll deliver a hodgepodge of all the above. The looks on their faces and their retching sounds will be a sure-fire guarantee—one less eating adventure to worry about. The slugs of the world will be safe!

Mealtime is playtime and playtime is mealtime. Your job as *Mealtime Referee* will be firmly established. The games are on! Opposing sides line up for the scrimmage. The stakes are high! The games and rules change by the minute! Creativity is at its peak! Whether it's *Spaghetti-Tug-of-War* or *Food-Fight-with-Mush!*, the Super Bowl of food games happens at every meal, five times a day, 472 days a year. This comes to at least 2,360 food fights every 12 months. You will literally *cry* over spilled milk.

Your objective is to keep most of the food on the table and directed toward your kids' mouths. You need to keep milk in their glasses, their hands out of each other's food, and make sure each kid has *his own* food in front of him. To fulfill your obligations as *Mealtime Referee*, you'll have your own play list of audibles that sounds like this:

Joey: "He sdarded it!"

You: "I don't care who started it. Just eat!"

Joey: "But dhats my mlk!"

You: "I don't care! Drink this milk!"

Mikey: "Btdhats my mlk!"

You: "I don't care!! Drink dthis milk dthen!"

Samuel: "But dhats mine!"

You: "I don't care! Djust eat!

Joey: "But he sdarded it!"

Samuel: "No I dint! Dyou did!"

You: "I DON'T CARE! DJUST DEAT! OR YOU'LL NEVER DEAT AGAIN!!"

While the games may be different, it's the same story for every meal. Day after day, week after week, month after month, year after year... The only thing that stops you from slamming the plates down on the table and screaming, "Go ahead and eat each other for all I care!" is your fear of being completely drummed out of the *Mealtime Ref's Association*. Or, you go ahead and threaten to do yourself in by beating your head in with the peanut butter & jelly sandwich you found stuck in the screen door! The kids love that one.

In any case, your antics will be completely void of anything resembling rational thought. Whether you're a dad or a mom, the kids will get a kick out of watching an unshaven, too-tired-to-think, wild person—dressed only in underwear—frantically waving the spatula at the wannabe-*Galloping Gourmet*-dog, who's lapping up syrup off of your screaming one-year-old! You and the dog have become the kids' very own nonstop, live streaming cartoon show. Wonderful.

Eventually, they become toddlers, and will be much more creative and independent. Their bedrooms become full-blown kitchens with pantries. It's not uncommon to discover two or three boxes of *Cream of Wheat*, a gallon of milk and a five-pound bag of kitty litter poured all over their carpets, their beds, and their heads. If cereal isn't on the menu for that morning, your little "gourmands" might prepare, for example, raw eggs blended with pancake mix and bath water. Of course, a bed makes for a perfect mixing bowl, which brings a whole new meaning to *Breakfast In Bed*.

Sneaking into the bathroom for a half a minute will be your downfall. In this nanosecond, kids can coordinate, and then conduct, their kitchen raiding maneuvers. Whenever you hear the sounds of eggbeaters, spoons, whisks, giggling, and the pitter-patter of little feet, you can be certain—*disaster is in the making*. The sounds of the blender on "purée" will kick your stimulus-response mechanism into high gear!

Super Parent leaps into action faster than a speeding bullet! You grab the broom and mop from the hallway closet *(as well as the neighbor's power-washer from his backyard)*, and race through clouds of flour to discover that, indeed, gourmet creativity had gone terribly wrong! Not only is their mealtime concoction dripping from the ceilings, the walls, and bunk beds, it's also pooling in the carpets, pillows, and blankets! The dog races past you as a white blur, not even considering using his lapping skills to help with the cleanup. Railing at the powers to be, you shake your mop in the air yelling, "Why me, why me, why me?!"

Because the kids are so young, the concept of, "cleaning up" escapes their collective consciousness—*but not yours!* Playtime/

mealtime reaches new heights. They'll have just as much fun watching their personal valet *(you)* throw a fit–while frothing, slopping, and dancing hysterically from one end of their bedroom to the other on a carpet of vinegar-drenched cornflakes and freshly cracked eggs! It's all you can do to salvage any remaining food for their breakfast–which they still haven't yet eaten!

It's true–you want them to become self-sufficient as soon as possible; however, you'll need to brace yourself for the out-of-mind *(and out-of-pocket)* onslaught: when they decide to take over the cooking responsibilities altogether. Make no mistake–between the peanut butter & ketchup sandwiches, the crackers & macaroni soufflés, and the cream-of-fish-stick soup dripping down the cupboards and drawers, your impatience and insane rantings *will* get the best of you. So, once again, you'll find solace in your *Twiddly-Lips* corner, muttering the mantra of your moment-to-moment prayer: *"God save me! Oh God, please save me!"*

This is not to mention whenever you open the milk container to pour your guests cream for their coffee, it becomes a guessing game to figure out just what exactly seems to be slithering to the surface for air. It could be anything from stink-bug flavored milk to the other half of that slug for all you know! The fact that these surprises slowly become "normal," pushes you further and further into the depths of parental delirium.

And then… comes… dinner time. This is usually the part of the day when you've finally reached your boiling point. You'll be opening the umpteenth can of tuna fish with one hand, while shaking the index finger of your other hand at your five-year-old, yelling, "IT'S ME OR YOU! IT'S ME OR YOU!!"

And right smack in the middle of these pinnacle power struggles, as if on cue, your two-and-a-half-year-old will inevitably come to you like an angel with wings and a halo, carrying a half-broken dandelion, looking for praise and acceptance. At the same exact time you're condemning one child to a fate far too disturbing to put in writing, you'll be graciously accepting the gift of "innocent and pure" love of another child. Can you say, "Berserk"?

It's during these maniacal moments that your over-caffeinated imagination will reach out and drag you back into its seething cesspool of self-imprisoning questions and other mental debris. *Do they plan this stuff? Are they really a team with an agenda? Is there a conspiracy going on here? Did the brother-in-trouble summon the "angel" in to finger-block?* Before you can even begin to decipher this vast array of self-imposed, mind-boggling interrogations, you'll be interrupted with…

- A robotic-like human phone solicitor who actually hangs up on you because she can't take your whining anymore;
- A cat duct-taped to a football flying past your face;
- The neighbor's kid crying because he has a sliver in his foot; and
- Electrifying jolts of pain zig-zagging throughout your body from the stubbed toe you just suffered while sprinting, dodging, and cart wheeling your way across the kitchen to save what *was* going to be the family dinner.

By now *(30 seconds later)*, you've completely forgotten about the kid you were going to have drawn and quartered, the robotic phone solicitor who keeps hanging up on you, and everything else

for that matter. It really hits you! You see the light! This is it! You have just lost the house to a blur of rambunctious kids, all their friends, a wannabe-show-dog, and a roll of duct tape. You've been cooked, fried, sautéed, roasted, and skewered. In other words, put a fork in it–you're done.

You go to the nearest window and jump. Since the window happens to be on the first floor, you quickly realize it's gonna take a couple more jumps than you originally anticipated. So, you kiss your life's goals and dreams goodbye, and resort to playing *Twiddly-Lips* in your favorite corner instead.

However, on the way to your haven, you're confronted with three, *He-Hit-Me-First* games, a loose parakeet, the neighbor's kid with another sliver in his foot, that flying cat, and if you're married, a, "Honey I'm home… What's for dinner?"

This *is* the routine. There *are* no breaks. *None.* Even if you do get a chance to hire a babysitter—so you can go hang out with the neighbor's cat on the porch, or something wild and crazy like that—like most parents you'll be confined, restricted, and bound to the overall responsibilities connected to the three-ring-circus carrying on inside your house.

These ongoing daily escapades begin to rip away at all of your lifelong dreams. You'll go into the bathroom, sit on your *Ivory Tower of Introspection*, and face up to the unfathomable. Life will stare you in the face and reality is its relentless encore—a dream-crashing reality: all these kids and a wannabe-show-dog. You either suffer from ADHD ("A Dad Had Dreams"), or AMHD ("A Mom Had Dreams"), or MADD ("Mom and Dad Disorder"). In any case, this is a hard pill to swallow.

In that life-altering, earthshaking moment, it all hits you. There's no way around it. You're a parent now. Whether you like it or not, you *will* be vicariously fulfilled!

Yay! That's the spirit!

> "No one's raising children any more. To love a child, you've got to work for it. You have to change its diapers and feed it at night!"
>
> LAUREN HUTTON

4

BATH TIME

As I was shaving one morning, I couldn't help but notice just how thoughtful two-year-olds could really be. With the determined force and whirlwind of a little tornado, my child had decided to scrub the family toilet to a sparkling shine. With utmost care and attention to detail, he scrubbed and scoured and splashed his way under the rim, around the bowl and as deep as he could possibly reach. I felt very proud of my industrious little beaver as he tackled this project head-on, and with such vigor!

Then, all of a sudden, I jolted back into a very harsh and somewhat frantic reality. This little guy was cleaning and scouring the toilet—with my toothbrush!

Not being what it once was, my kaleidoscope mind took all this in from a slightly different angle. Because he was doing such a good job—and, quite frankly, better than I'd ever done—it dawned on me: this might not have been the first time he had cleaned the toilet with my toothbrush. My next thought, of course, was that this child has older brothers who, at one time, had been "thoughtful" two-year-olds themselves. So... how long had I been brushing my teeth with the kids' toilet brush?!

Along with the usual soapy eyes, head dunking, and bath toys, your bathroom becomes a tsunami of flying elbows, waves of, "He's splashing me!" and swim competitions. The inventiveness of your clever young "water squirts" brings new meaning to the words, "bath time."

Since you spend so much time in the tub cleaning up—after breakfast, long days of playing outside, and pre-bedtime pee fights, you'll be under the misguided delusion that it's your responsibility to make bath time a happy time. Initially, you will supply the common bath toys: rubber ducks, bouncing balls, fish, and anything else that floats. Unfortunately, most kids have their *own* bath time toys—and agendas.

As a general rule, "If it belongs in the tub, it won't be in the tub." Instead, the bath toys will be dangling and strewn from one end of your neighbor's roof to the other, or, even better yet, duct-taped to the dog to see if he floats.

On the other hand, if it doesn't belong in the bathtub, it will, of course, be in the tub. Along with the older brothers' chemistry set and your last six years of tax returns, their favorite bath toys are typically the "real" toilet brush, your tool box, and an occasional bag of dog food *(or two)*.

Since bath time is just another game to push the remaining sanity of any still-standing parental figure over the edge, the kids will figure it out: the more "toys" they bring into the bathtub, the more fun they'll have. This will also include using mom's makeup to paint funny faces on the mirror and paint racing stripes on the sink, bathtub, and walls—not to mention all over themselves and each other—thus initiating their careers in, *Graffiti Painting!*

As the kids grow older, the tub gets smaller. Bath time escalates into the game of, *Bathroom Remodel!* Yay! You'll hopelessly negotiate with yourself as to whether you're going to have to give up your arm, your leg, or your firstborn—in order to replace the water-logged and buckled linoleum floor.

Like the *Twiddly-Lips* corner, the bathroom will become your only other means of escape. Your *Ivory Tower of Escape.* Even then, as if on cue, your phone will telepathically know when you're in there. Normally, you'd let it ring to its heart's content, but if you're expecting a very important phone call like I was one fine day, you'll know you have no choice but to drop everything you're doing—pun not intended—and answer it.

In my case, I was expecting an important call and had to answer it. I reached for the universal necessity—toilet paper—but found nothing. Looking around frantically, my eyes zeroed in on islands of white, soggy, and disintegrating toilet paper floating in the tub—*my children's latest bath toys*—not one, but two, rolls of toilet paper.

To answer the phone or not, *that* was the question. My moment of solace was gone. With or without any toilet paper, I had to reach the phone. I couldn't miss that important call—not to mention the added bonus of speaking to someone over the age of 10!

The game was on: Get a new roll of toilet paper from the hallway cupboard, swing back by the bathroom, and then answer the phone before it stopped ringing. This was a tough play, but I had to do it!

With my attention somewhat diverted because the screaming kids had decided to answer the phone which was then causing the answering machine to feedback (again, this was back in the early '80s when we depended on land lines and answering machines), I initiated my game plan: quickly sneak, wobble, and stumble my way down the hall to the cupboard with my underwear and pants wrapped around my ankles. Winded and panic-stricken, I grasped the cupboard door, flung it open, and well, what do you know? No toilet paper!

Hopping, tripping, and cussing, I then square-danced my way back up the hall to a now fully occupied and locked bathroom. As a vast array of colorful words ricocheted and reverberated throughout every room in the house *(and across the street)*, I was interrupted by a viciously rude and belligerent, "Daddy! Daddy! Daddy!" echoing directly behind me.

Flailing, and kicking, and convulsing at the bathroom door like a lassoed rodeo calf, and with fire and brimstone combusting and exploding out of my nostrils, I turned around and replied with, "NOW WHAT?? !#*!^?!* CAN'T YOU SEE I'M !#*!^?!* BUSY?!!!" only to see that my halo-bearing three-year-old had graciously welcomed our neighborhood group of Jehovah's Witnesses into our living room...

Today's sermon? "How too many people aren't ready for the Lord when He comes knocking at their door."

Amen.

"Bathtime is successful when your kids get wetter than you do."

DEE ANN STEWART
(WHAT SPOCK FORGOT)

"Diaper backward spells repaid. Think about it."

MARSHALL McLUHAN

5

POTTY TRAINING

Potty training should be called *Parent Training*, because when it's time to go, it's time to go! You have a vested interest in this activity, because the sooner you get the kid out of diapers, the more independent he will be and the more independent *you* will be. However, the process of getting your kid out of diapers and onto the toilet is the Supreme Gauntlet thrown down by the Gods to see when you will lose the last bit of your sanity. Potty training can be the ultimate test in patience. Ah, that word again, patience: **The bearing of provocation, annoyance, and pain without complaint, irritation, or loss of temper...**

The typical potty training episode usually starts out with you chasing your own bladder down the hall because *you* waited too long to go. Before you even get to the bathroom, however, you'll get trapped into refereeing the older kids' game of, *Tug-of-War* with the neighbor's cat, grabbing scissors out of someone's hands, and jumping into the laundry room to wrestle an out-of-control, off-balance washing machine, which is bouncing, buzzing, and dancing its way across the linoleum floor and halfway out the window! In your continuous dialog with those above, you look skyward and say, "You guys are funny."

Before you can save the neighbor's cat from losing one of its nine lives, and lasso the bucking bronco washing machine before it jumps out the window, your bladder reminds you it's about to burst. Lunging into the bathroom to cater to your own pressing needs, you find yourself face-to-face with your potty "trainee" standing knee-deep in the toilet with his sopping wet pants wrapped around his ankles and feet, like Chinese handcuffs.

God only knows what's smeared up and down the rest of his body! "Is that tarred sawdust?" you query. The smell alone knocks you straight into another time zone. As usual, there's no sign of toilet paper for 300 yards, but you quickly realize it wouldn't do much good anyway. This contamination field of biohazard requires the use of a pneumatic chisel, a HAZMAT suit, and a HAZARDOUS WASTE permit from the Environmental Protection Agency!

The second issue with potty training, if you have boys, is, *Aim!* You wonder if painting a bull's-eye in the toilet bowl would do the trick. Fortunately, the problem of aim is temporary. Once hitting their mark is achieved, they'll soon be up to their usual creative

learning standards of writing their names in the snow and chasing each other around the house having pee fights.

The third issue with boys, is every once in a while, they will get their "peters" caught in their pants' zippers. There's no mistaking the high-pitched supersonic waves of distress resonating from the GPS system that alerts you to this catastrophic tight spot. It doesn't matter if you're in the middle of changing a diaper, cooking breakfast, or fighting the dog for the TV remote, this five-star red alert demands *immediate attention!*

"Peters" caught in zippers is a *Catch 22* dilemma. There are two opposing, yet equal goals. On one hand, the kid has GOT to be freed, but on the other hand, and under absolutely NO circumstance, does he allow you to touch him. You don't know whether to pull the zipper up? Or down? This depends on whether he was about to go potty or had just finished. He can't remember. All he knows is he desperately needs someone to calmly and quietly, with surgical precision, separate the delicate skin from the teeth of the zipper.

Instead, he's confronted with a hideously possessed, mentally-crazed, fire-spitting giant gargoyle *(you)*, whose glaring bloodshot eyes are sunken into a hollow, smoldering, steaming skull (from lack of sleep because the newborn kept everyone up for the last three straight nights)! The veins in your forehead, nose, and neck are venomously pulsating with each and every convulsing breath, after ranting, raving, and frothing across the house hysterically screaming and shouting, "NOW WHAT??! #*!^?!* REALLY??! #%!!*^!! ARE YOU #*!^?!*ING KIDDING ME???!!! #!%*>!!! WHAT THE #!%*>!!! IS THE PROBLEM???!!! GOD SAVE US!! 'CAUSE IF I HAD A BUTTON I'D NUKE US ALL!!"

Uhh... yeah.

Now that the kid is in an absolute state of shock, and half unconscious from the pain, everything he sees, hears, and smells becomes implanted into his subconscious as a hypnotic command. 50 years later, when he becomes the President of the United States and finds himself walking down the hall in the West Wing with his top advisers to decide the fate of the world, he coincidentally runs into his three-year-old grandson, who's frantically screaming because he's got his "peter" caught in his zipper! This, of course, re-stimulates your son, "The President," to suddenly, and without warning, transform into a "hideously possessed, mentally-crazed, fire-spitting giant gargoyle... ranting and raving and frothing across the White House screaming, "NOW WHAT??! #*!^?!* REALLY??! #%!!*^!! ARE YOU #*!^?!*ING KIDDING ME???!!! #!%*>!!! WHAT THE #!%*>!!! IS THE PROBLEM???!!! GOD SAVE US!! 'CAUSE IF I HAD A BUTTON I'D NUKE US ALL!!"

Sorry... got carried away. The point is, potty training is important.

THE POTTY SONG

Tinkle, Tinkle Little Star
Down the toilet very far.
Flush it down, round & round
Now close the lid without a sound
Tinkle, Tinkle Little Star
Someday you will know
How proud we are.

RONNY MUNROE

"Necessity may be the mother of invention, but play is certainly the father."

ROGER VON OECH
(PRESIDENT, CREATIVE THINK)

6
PLAY TIME

To a three-year-old mind, the word "share" is utterly incomprehensible. As far as kids are concerned, it might as well mean, "Mine! Mine! Mine! And ONLY mine!"

Playtime activities are basically a series of small battles, which often escalate into full-scale wars of such magnitude that you would gladly join the French Foreign Legion–if only they'd return your calls. In fact, a parent really has less of a chance of navigating through the front lines of this type of battle than General Custer did at his Last Stand.

When those consciousness-altering, brain-blistering screams reach your supersonically-tuned ears, you'll leap tall buildings with a single bound and jump directly into the fray to repo the toy from the whole lot!

If your kids and their friends are all fighting over the only Big Wheel on the block, you've just unwittingly signed up as the *Neighborhood Referee*. And if, by chance, the Big Wheel happens to belong to a three-year-old, goooooood luck! The "Mine! Mine! Mine! And ONLY mine!" theory of sharing kicks the screams up 1,200 decibels to 30,000 watts of eardrum-shattering, out-of-control microphone feedback! These hypersonic waves can actually send vibrations so devastating to your ears that any attempt at rational thought is immediately excused as "nonsense" and replaced with a kamikaze urge to apply duct tape to everything in sight!

Remember, in the Pre-Ramble I said, "Kids are people too and should be treated with respect..."? FORGET IT!

You arrive at the scene, half-unconscious and fully-delirious from the brain-blistering pain. At one quick glance, you realize the battle is in high gear. The lines of demarcation have been clearly drawn. The frantic three-year-old is grasping with all his might, trying to hold onto what he truly believes is an extension of his life! For him, having control of this Big Wheel IS life or death.

As the *Neighborhood Referee*, law and order must be restored! In a single glance, you quickly size up the battle, give the Big Wheel to the three-year-old, and threaten to hog-tie anyone who tries to take away his toy!

Your judge and jury stance may not win a popularity contest with the older kids, but you forfeit being popular in order to stop the ear-piercing screeches from penetrating every cell of your sleep-deprived, caffeine-depleted body! Unfortunately, fighting is a daily ritual for kids, and if you try to stop them, you'd be depriving them of what they consider to be a healthy sport. Even though peace is restored, realize it only lasts as long as it takes for the little diablos to pick up another toy—three seconds.

Having a large family redefines your living quarters as the "neighborhood's playground." No matter how much screaming, yelling, and crying you do, the kids will simply disregard your nervous breakdowns and continue running in and out, up and down, and back and forth—dragging their war-beaten toys throughout your living room, dining room, bathroom, and kitchen. Your entire house will become one big "wrecked room" and your front entrance becomes a revolving door.

It's not uncommon to find kids you've never seen before raiding your refrigerator, so you may as well put a revolving door on that too!

"It is not a parent's job to protect their kids from life, but to prepare them for it."

BLAKE SEGAL

7

CHILD PROOFING

Child proofing is also known as, *You vs. Them.* It pushes your sanity to the nth degree and keeps you in a *never-ending, knee-jerking, drop everything, and scramble toward the screams no matter what* mode. You'll be on watch, on guard, and on auto-pilot. Every minute of every day, year in and year out. Screams are the enemy, and when they happen, you'll be on them, faster than a speeding bullet!

With a revolving front door and umpteen kids constantly running in and out and from one end of the house to the other, the risk factor for a catastrophe is off the charts! As the 28-hour-a-day *Resident Safety Inspector*, you'll find it next to impossible to fully childproof your home. Unless you attach rubber bumpers to everything—including the kids—and spend every waking *(and not-so-waking)* hour protecting them with giant fire-retardant marshmallows and bulletproof pillows, child proofing is a pipe dream for another time and dimension.

The term "creative genius" is another way of saying, "a catastrophe waiting to happen." It doesn't take long for a two-year-old to become a mountain climbing engineer in order to figure out how to defy the laws of gravity just enough to teeter a tower of chairs up to the ceiling so he can then play *Spiderman*.

Most boys will invent ways to rewire the kitchen, build a tree house on the roof of the car, light the carpet on fire with a magnifying glass, or build dirt tracks in the living room to play *Demolition Derby* three months before they are even out of the womb. Although silence can be golden, you know a sudden burst of quiet means a nuclear attack is about to happen.

As usual, the bathroom is your downfall. Thirty seconds of solitude means that the house could blow at any minute. In the time it takes for you to go to your *Ivory Tower of Introspection*, your kids can become spellbound with such things as:

- Putting their arms in the washing machine—while it's running;
- Cutting five inch strips in the curtains;
- Ironing the carpet;
- Dismantling the fan—while it's running;
- Sticking bubble gum in each other's hair;
- Digging holes in the backyard with your cutlery set;
- Filling up the gas tank with the garden hose;
- Roller-skating up and down the stairs;
- Playing with the older brother's chemistry set;
- Teetering in 30-foot-high treetops;
- Competing to see how many marbles they can stuff into their mouths;
- Sticking screwdrivers in the electrical outlets;
- Climbing out of the upstairs windows to play *Tag!* on the roof;
- Climbing up the tree to swing on the telephone lines;

- Setting off fireworks in the house; and
- Probably two zillion other things you don't want to know about.

Child proofing is similar to the game, Simon Says. You remember—Simon says, "Do this," and everyone does. Well, the game of, Child Proofing is the same as Simon Says, but in reverse. It's as if the word, "DON'T" never existed. And it goes like this:

What you say: "Don't jump on the bed!"
What they hear: "Jump on the bed!"
What you say: "Don't climb on that 3,000,000-volt electric fence!"
What they hear: "Climb on that 3,000,000-volt electric fence!"
What you say: "Don't poke your brother's eye out with that stick!"
What they hear: "Poke your brother's eye out with that stick!"

When urgency is a factor, their frantic discordant symphony chimes in:

Them: "Hdyr*ntudtehrt#asunrhd78irkjr!uidysg!"
You: "One at a time!"
Them: "Hdyrntudte*hrtasunrhd78i#rkjruidy!sg!"
You: "I said one at a time!"
Them: "Hdyrntudtehrtasunr*hd78irkjrui#dysg!"

On top of these inconveniences are the usual: etching their names into the side of a car with the only writing tool available—a nail; using the neighbor's window for target practice with a rock; treating the backseat of the car as their personal barf bucket whenever it's time to get car sick; and so on.

This is not to mention one of your favorite hobbies: unclogging your toilet! Unclogging the toilet is always a fun one. After three days of splashing your hands and face in toilet water, the toilet is still no closer to being unclogged than it was when you first started. You have no choice but to rip it out of the floor and turn it over and over again until the stuffed animal, toy soldier, or your great grandpa's antique watch falls out.

Being the *Resident Safety Inspector*, you are on guard every millisecond of every day, eight days a week. You wait with bated breath, bracing yourself for what extra delight the universe might throw your way any second.

Keeping track of kids is like corralling cats. They're constantly running in all directions. This brings up the question: How is it possible for a two-and-a-half-year-old to disappear so quickly? One instant he's tying his toy train set around your feet as you're cooking breakfast and then **POOF!** The next second he's gone. Absolutely gone! Where did he go?!

Even though you hunger and long for peace and quiet, the *Protector Parent* side of your brain kicks in. Q-U-I-E-T spells T-R-O-U-B-L-E. This means anything from priming fireworks under a bed, to a surprise visit from Grandma and Grandpa! Your extrasensory radar ears go into overdrive!

Operation: Find the Kid is in full force. Your anxious reconnaissance work has you dividing the house into quarters, calling the kid's name and even asking your wannabe-*Sherlock Holmes*-dog if he's seen him. No answer. He's too busy licking his butt. Unease creeps up your spine. Not a peep. The kid is simply *gone!*

Knowing full well there's no way on this God-forsaken, holographic planet the kid had time to gather all his belongings, erase his DNA, and walk out the back door, you have no choice but to stagger outside to check anyway. Nothing. Where in heaven's name did he go? You quickly make your way to the back yard where two of his brothers are playing. They haven't seen him either! Around the perimeter of the house you go. Nothing! Over and through the front yard and then the back again. Nothing! The only signs of life are you and the dog...

Suddenly, without rhyme or reason, out of the corner of your eye, you swear you've just seen the top of the kid's head bounce up above the neighbor's backyard three-and-a-half houses away. Impossible. Time travel? Teleportation? Time jumping? Despite the laws of physics, and every known and unknown string theory preventing such a concept, he *is* in fact *there*, playing as though he has been there all day!

It has to be true—and it is true—an obvious black hole in time and space. What else could a normal, mentally-deranged parent think?

This also leads you to wonder how the reverse could be possible. How do those kids know when you're finally getting the chance to enjoy that Haagen-Daz ice-cream bar you'd managed to keep hidden in the back of the freezer? They could be playing on the other side of the Milky Way Galaxy, and before you can get the wrapper off, they're hopping around your feet with smiles of anticipatory glee across their faces. How do they do that?

Again . . . Time travel, teleportation, black holes, and mental vortexes. There are no other explanations.

> "Silence is golden. Unless you have kids, then silence is just suspicious!"
>
> UNKNOWN

8

ALONG COME PETS

In addition to the usual rearing of children, a family may find themselves invaded by pets. Big pets, little pets, orange pets . . . and dogs.

If you find keeping the kids from continuously letting the wing-clipped parakeets, gerbils, and stick insects out of their cages for the cat to chase isn't stimulating enough, you may consider getting a dog too. Not a cute little puppy for the kids to grow up and play with, but something resembling a fully grown, red-haired, greyhound-looking, wannabe-show-dog! They are MUCH more entertaining!

This dog's needs and wants have absolutely nothing to do with being tied up to a house for the purpose of getting kicked, pinched, bitten, and choked into unconsciousness every other minute by a horde of wild, wrangling renegades.

You won't know whose nerves will get the worst of it, the dogs or yours. If you can imagine spending 110% of your time protecting a dog from having its ears cut off with a pair of scissors or being tied up like a rodeo calf and then strangled by its leash, you might get the picture. Your "prayer" will change to, *"God save me and the dog! Oh God. PLEASE save me and the dog!"*

It also quickly becomes apparent that your dog will go to great lengths to let the City Council know whenever a neighborhood cat sets a paw in your yard, by yelping and charging his way through the family's dinner table, and up and down the living room sofa! If you just happen to live next door to a cat factory where felines are being cranked out by the thousands, this ritual will provide you with a never-ending source of robust entertainment.

Don't forget, you can't have pets without having FLEAS! Fleas are an integral part of owning pets. Fleas/pets! Pets/fleas! Fleas/pets! Next to the 2 a.m. mosquito, fleas are the most disgusting, relentless, cantankerous, ridiculous forms of blood sucking, parasitic havoc there are.You'll quickly learn there are two types of flea care: Preventative Flea Care and *It's-Too-Late Flea Care.*

The first option, *Preventative Flea Care,* is self-explanatory and very, very simple. FOR THE LOVE OF ALL THAT IS HOLY, DO NOT HAVE PETS!!!

The second option, *It's-Too-Late Flea Care,* begins with, "REALLY??! #%!!*^!! ARE YOU ^#!%* KIDDING ME???!!! #!%*>!!! NO FRICKIN' WAY!!!!" And always ends with you chasing the kids, the dog, the cat, and some birds around the house six times—wildly swinging a half-changed, wet, poopy diaper at them—because it's obviously *their* fault!

The first thing you want to do (but can't because it usually attracts too much attention, and attention is the *last* thing you need), is to take everything out of the house, pour gasoline on it, and burn it to the ground—twice. Instead, you have no choice but to pull everything in the house away from the walls in order to vacuum, spray, spray, vacuum, spray, vacuum, vacuum, and spray every centimeter of the base of all the walls.

After you've vacuumed your mattresses, carpets, upholstery, floors, dog, car, lawn, sidewalk, cat, birdhouse, tree-house, drapes, birds, roof—and the kids—you'll need to get rid of the vacuum bag immediately! (And, for God's sake, DO NOT dump it into your neighbor's yard as you usually do with the cat's litter box. Fleas come back and spawn!)

Next, wash all of your personal belongings, kids' toys, and bedding with *methyl ethyl ketone*... Er, I mean the hottest soap and water you can find. This is supposed to *(but doesn't)* kill off the fleas and their confounded immune-building-time-released eggs.

Finally, you can purchase a flea bomb or "indoor fogger" (they call it that because you can get pretty foggy after you breathe enough of it), and then wash any residue off of the surfaces of everything and vacuum all the above again... and again, and again.

You do have the option of calling in an exterminator at the start, but you're still going to have to do all the above before the professional's spray can do its job anyway.

In between homework, meals, naps, etc., etc., etc., ridding your house of fleas is a major pain in the butt! That "cute little puppy" in the pet store window, needs to STAY in the window. Let some other schmuck play the *Get Rid of Fleas* game! You have too much to do already and a lot better things with which to occupy your time!

> "We've begun to long for the pitterpatter of little feet—so we bought a dog. Well, it's cheaper, and you get more feet."
>
> RITA RUDNER

9
A DAY AT THE BEACH

A day at the beach is a great way to spend quality time with your kids. The beach offers sand, sun, water, kids, and you—a volatile combination.

The hunt for swimming trunks, beach balls, and the chewed-up Frisbee is on! Ransacking the house, digging up the back yard, and turning the neighborhood upside down, you frantically attempt to locate all these and other essential items—not to mention enough Valium to make the *Grateful Dead* even more grateful!

Why did you even mention to the kids about going to the beach? Oh, yeah, you were reactively looking for an infusion of sanity as you remembered it *before* you had kids. By the time the fights are settled over who gets to sit in the front seat, you're ready to go! Right? Wrong again!

Taking all of this in, with the most pitiful "what about me" look he can possibly muster is the dog—standing with his sad face glued to the front window. Putting the dog out of your mind and the car in reverse, you start to roll quietly and slowly down the driveway.

However, four inches down the driveway later, the dog's "poor me" look morphs into an all-knowing "got you" smirk. The dog's telepathic powers tractor beam directly to your screaming kids and car! Nobody, including the car, will let you leave without him. Wonderful...

Upon your arrival at the beach, you scope out a parking spot nearest the bathrooms. Before your hyper-kinetic, round'em-up, shoot'em-up kids can leap from your eyeshot, you dish out your umpteenth dissertation about why they should stay within the boundaries of the picnic area, which includes the usual visuals, audibles, and fingers-in-the-face signals. Within a millisecond of finishing, your kids scatter in every direction like exposed sea crabs to play in the radiant sea of sunburned flesh. Your *Super Parent Perceptions* go into full alert.

And there you are, with three zillion half-naked screaming kids running around, kicking sand and dirt into everyone else's picnic. From 20 feet away, they all look alike. This mayhem of boundless energy hyper-extends the neurosis of every caffeinated, neurotic, wild-eyed parent as they rush around trying to figure out which kid is or isn't theirs.

Keeping your eyes focused in "quadrant-vision," and your ears tuned in to the radar signals emanating from your specific offspring, you start unloading the car. With the dog leash in one hand and groceries in the other, you suddenly freeze. Your legs are paralyzed. The leash tightens. You can't move. "What the...?" Your wannabe-*Montie Montana*-dog has somehow managed to lasso the three-feet of dog leash six dozen times around your ankles, car bumper, and hibachi?! How does he do that?

With four rambunctious healthy boys at the beach, lunch hour comes early, and regularly. The signals are all there. It's time to

eat! Your four-year-old is glopping peanut butter & jelly up and down the dog's back, while the three-year-old is licking it off. Your one-year-old is crying because the dog is eating his Juicy Fruits and it's raining soda because your five-year-old has shaken up the can for your four-year-old to open.

After devouring as much peanut butter & jelly as possible, your three-year-old moves onto his second course: chewing gum he's found stuck underneath the picnic table. The dog is helping your four-year-old suck down his Cherry Popsicle, and the one-year-old is crying again because he *and* the dog want more Juicy Fruits. So, you give the dog a bottle.

And you haven't even finished unloading the car yet!

Whenever your dog has you bring him to the beach, you'll also need to prepare for every stray dog in a three-county radius to make a beeline out of the water, directly to your picnic table for their regular *Shake-Dance* and *Butt-Smelling Rituals*. They'll shake, spray, and douse water all over the peanut butter & jelly sandwiches, potato chips, and starving kids.

Next, you have to explain to the kids the other part of the rit-ual—butt-smelling. The reasons why dogs smell other dogs' butts are extremely precious, valuable, and can't-live-without pieces of information for three-year-olds!

Being the *Super Parent Know-It-All Dictionary* you are, you ex-plain:

You: "Smelling each others butts is a way for them to get to know each other."

Him: "Why?"

You: "Because they know things by their sense of smell."

Him: "Oh... You know what?"

You: "No, my enlightened son. What?"

Him: "You're spilling my pop."

So much for the *Super Parent Dictionary*.

When your beach day lasts into the evening, you continue your picnic with the family tradition of an open fire and barbecue. Nothing like the great taste of mouth-watering, sizzling, smoky hamburgers, and hot dogs with the occasional moth flapping across the hot pan of honey-glazed beans after a fun day at the beach!

Ah yes, who could ask for anything more? If you can keep their fingers out of the raw food long enough to grill it, you might have a meal. Fresh air and kids equals bringing lots of extra food. They'll eat anything and everything in sight.

Three lighters, two matchbooks, and a tanker truck of lighter fluid later, you finally get the "quick start" briquettes to stay lit! You know... the same briquettes that won't cool down until the next Ice Age, when you're *really* going to need them.

You are also joined by every mosquito within 300 galaxies! You'll notice those bug lights and sprays sold to kill mosquitoes are only a "Come and Get It!" solar beacon making them even more hungry! They fly in from their long journey to enjoy their evening smorgasbord—the insides of your ankles, knees, and el-

bows. Next to the rage-compelling, cantankerous fleas, mosquitoes rank a close second.

When the sun sets and the mosquitoes and kids run out of food—it's the all-defining signal to go home. Knowing the payoff—movies and ice cream—the kids can't get to the car fast enough.

After you unbelt the dog from the one-year-old's car seat—because the dog thinks he needs to be in it—and get all of the kids packed into the car, you are finally homeward bound.

The drive home consists mostly of you pulling over every 30 seconds to explain to the screeching kids that if they don't stop screaming, biting, and hitting, they won't get any ice cream. Completely ignoring your attempt at this "authoritative" bribe, the kids resume their frenzied wrestling, shouting, and horsing around as you bullet your tormented, overworked 1972 Grand Torino Station Wagon back into the "0-to-60mph-in-one-second" traffic.

Just as you enter your favorite "suicide" cloverleaf exit, your soda-pop-soaked, wannabe-*Mario Andretti*-dog decides it's his turn to drive again. In your rear-view mirror, you watch him leap and jump and frolic his way from the back of the station wagon, through all the screaming kids and eventually over your head to grab the steering wheel away from you.

You'd agree to the idea of letting him take over if he didn't always try to run over every stray cat he saw.

"Life is either a daring
adventure or nothing."

HELEN KELLER

10

SOCCER DAD

Somehow, between shuffling the kids to and from school, holding down a job or two, and constantly wrapping pillows around your personal belongings, your kids might become involved in sports. Being a proud sports parent of either several boys or girls, or both, requires having the ability to defy space and time by being at two or three games and/or practices, simultaneously.

Take soccer for example. As usual, there's a slight variation of what you picture happening before, during, and after games as compared to what actually takes place. Your game-week warm-up patter will go something like this:

Monday

> You: "Are your soccer clothes ready for your game on Saturday?"
> Them: "Yes."
> You: "Show me... Good."

Tuesday

> You: "Are you sure your soccer clothes are ready for your game on Saturday?"

"Do not throw in the towel; use it for wiping the sweat off your face."

UNKNOWN

Them: "Yes."

You: "Show me... Good."

Wednesday

You: "We are not going to have to look for soccer clothes on game day are we?"

Them: "No."

You: "Show me... Good."

Thursday

You: "You are positive your soccer clothes are ready for your game on Saturday?"

Them: "Yes."

You: "Show me... Good."

Friday

You: "Tomorrow is game day. Are your soccer clothes ready?"

Them: "Yes."

You: "Show me... Good."

Saturday

You: "Where are your soccer clothes?"

Them: "Hdyr*ntudtehrt#asunrhd78irkjr!uidysg!"

You: "Hdyr*ntudtehrt#asunrhd78irkjr!uidysg!"

For the next 30 minutes, the house becomes filled with the cacophonous sounds of you screaming, "ARE YOU !^#!%*ING KIDDING ME???!!! REALLY?! WHERE IN THE !^#!%* ARE YOUR !^#!%*ING CLOTHES?!!!"

The replies to your questions are always a continuous reverberation and bombardment of, "I DUNNO! SOMEONE MUSTA STOLE 'EM!"

The roof, the neighbor's backyard, and the refrigerator will become the typical storage places for lost uniforms, shin guards, and soccer shoes. Once the half-chewed soccer shoes, mud-caked shin guards, and petrified jerseys are presumably found, phase one of your *Pre-Game* show is over.

Phase two starts with, "Everyone, let's go!" Then, "Everyone in the car, now!" Then, "I'm leaving without you! Let's go!" This is followed by a blur of bodies fighting over who gets the front seat. Once everybody is strapped in, away you go! You drive down the street waving goodbye to all your neighbors who've lined up to watch the show. You're certain they hold festivals celebrating every time you leave—or they finally get some sleep.

As soon as you arrive at the soccer field—along with all of the other cars full of frustrated and foggy-eyed, deranged-beyond-belief parents—your kids will find it necessary to remind you:

- There's no game that day;
- The game is somewhere else;
- It's your turn to bring the refreshments; or
- All the above.

Oh yeah! This is it! Game on! All those consuming moments: Shouting kids! Soccer balls flying! Adrenalin pumping! Everyone's shouting at the referee! The world could stop spinning and you wouldn't even notice. You'll vicariously experience every kick, elbow-to-the-groin, run, whistle, off-sides, block, out-of-bounds, goal, missed goal, and foul. This is what every sports-minded parent lives for! Yay!

WARNING: Your younger kids may not be all that thrilled or

interested in their older sibling's game. PARENT BEWARE—especially if you were in too much of a hurry to put on your own underwear and socks, like I was one time—WATCH OUT!

One game day, two of my children got bored and decided to concoct their own sideline entertainment. Synchronized with the precision and execution of MI6's finest, the little operatives snuck up behind me—and yanked my sweatpants down to my ankles.

Cool air, bare skin... First reaction? Out-of-body experience. Underwear? What underwear? Nanoseconds seemed like three hours. Three hours seemed like three years. Three years seemed like an eternity... Everything went into s - l - o - w   m - o - t - i - o - n.

What to do, what to do, what to do? Well... I guess I could either...

1. Play a rigorous game of *Tug-of-War* with my kids clutching my sweats like it was a lifeline; or
2. Continue to watch the game with a resigned, *"What's the use?"* shrug.

My life passed before my eyes. I watched my mind vacillate between these two monumental schools of thought. My fingers began to tingle. I couldn't breathe. A vibration buzzed in my head. Sounds washed in. Sounds washed out. The words, "do something" swirled and drifted like falling leaves around the periphery of my catatonic mind—or what was left of it.

Although I couldn't quite put it all together, I was pretty sure I'd just been abducted by aliens. The tingling sensations in my hands had now turned into heat waves of vibrations running up my arms, across my chest, and up to my face. As my head slowly tipped forward, my eyes began to focus on what appeared to be a pair of white boney knees. A voice in my head said, "Hey, I recognize those knees..."

Just beyond said knees, my focus shifted to a couple of hysterical children, clinging to what appeared to be my sweats. They were rolling around on top of each other and laughing so hard they were about to pee their pants! Another voice entered my fogged mind, "Hey, I recognize those kids..."

Their out-of-control heckling slowly gave way to sounds in the distance of kids screaming, "Kick the ball! Kick the ball!" The smells of freshly cut grass and dirt began to creep in. Commotion was all around. All of a sudden, it hit me! I was 100% exposed!

As I came to, I began to analyze the situation and couldn't help but to notice that every mother within eye shot was covering the eyes of any child within reach. An overpowering wisdom took over, and I concluded that their *Pull-Down-Sweats* game probably wasn't quite "politically correct" enough for this family-oriented event. With what little—and I mean little—dignity I had left, I decided to go with Option #1: "Play a rigorous game of, *Tug-of-War* with my kids clutching my sweats..."

I reached down, grabbed hold of my sweatpants and fought, and tugged, and fought, and tugged, some more. My little pranksters were laughing so hard they finally let go of my pants and grabbed their stomachs instead. In a reactive attempt to preserve my pride and dignity, I swiftly and as nonchalantly as possible re-covered myself with a smoothness that would rival 007 himself.

Most parents don't just sit back and watch the game play out. They bypass the coach at every play. In other words, youth soccer consists of approximately 33 sideline "coaches" screaming at their kids. "Kick the ball! Kick the ball! Kick the ball!" The substitute coach does his best to control his temper. Half of the players look like a bunch of clumsy, comatose zombies completely oblivious to the events of the game at play. The rest of them chase each other around the field wondering where the ball went.

Like the rambunctious, inventive kids they are, your children learn their soccer positions with the ease of an All-Star Pro.

Your eight-year-old might love paying goalie. His aim will get to be pretty darn accurate. Don't be surprised if one afternoon he completes what would have been a 60-yard punt directly into the attacking forward's groin. The fathers on the sidelines will immediately, collectively, and simultaneously drop to their knees in harrowing empathetic pain. This event proves to be another high-C note moment in the life of fatherhood!

As your children grow older and more mature, their games will become a lot more cerebral. Their thought patterns and ideas will blossom into radiant sculptures of scientific innovation and scholarly excellence. You begin to think this stage of mental development would be a great study for scientists at MIT. In fact, their creative engineering theories and experiments might even land them a full scholarship at a very early age. Who knows? Why not?

As an example of this phenomenal neuro-synaptic evolution, one afternoon I walked out on to my back patio for a quick breath of fresh air. I could hear the kids yelling and screaming in their usual playful ways. As I stepped outside, I noticed at my feet a nicely organized pile of... slithering slugs? "Huh? How could this be?" I mused. "Was there a slug convention in town? Was our lawn somehow tastier than the grass in the neighbor's yard? I thought we were done with slugs!?"

While my wandering thoughts were traveling down that lane, my eight-year-old zoomed past me at an unexaggerated 300 knots with his 10-year-old brother hot on his heels. Without breaking stride, and with the accuracy of a stealth bomber, the 10-year-old reached down, mid-flight, scooped up a handful of the slugs, and rocketed them directly at his target—the back of the eight-year-old's head.

As *Omniscient Narrator, Parent-in-the-Know*, my experiential knowledge has proven that, 93.7% of all slugs hurled as missiles will explode *immediately* upon impact. 82.6% of these slugs splatter into hundreds of pieces before slithering down the head and back of the designated target.

My eight-year-old, of course, had his own stockpile of slugs. The *Slimy-Slug-War* was on!

"Always be nice to your children because they are the ones who will choose your rest home."

PHYLLIS DILLER

11

SHOPPING

In short, pulling the SST Concorde out of mothballs and putting a pack of rabid dogs in the cockpit with Freddy Krueger
as the pilot on a flight to a Paris boutique shop, and then back
home again, would prove less challenging than taking all of your
kids to the grocery store. In other words, going to the store is the
ultimate **NIGHTMARE**!

After two hours of trying to convince yourself you really don't
need to go to the store *(and having used the last of your Sunday
Tribune as toilet paper...)*, you seriously consider cannibalism as a
lunchtime alternative. No food. No toilet paper.

Defeated, you finally surrender to the inevitable fact that you
must go to the store—immediately. *The Grocery Store Battle* is on!
Yay.

Worried about your parental image, you make sure your kids
are dressed in the cleanest clothes possible. You spend the next
hour-and-a-half searching for lost shoes—which is a whole chapter
in and of itself. Like everything else, shoes will never be in a place
where any half-sane parent would dare look. Being a mentally-deranged, caffeine-depleted parent doesn't really help either.

After dressing and redressing the kids twice *(just because)*, you make your way out to the family car—the 1972 Grand Torino Station Wagon, which is trying its earnest, yet pitiful attempt to hide. For the next 15 minutes, you'll play the skill-challenging game of, *Where-Are-the-Seat-Belts?!* This game involves ripping all of the seats apart with one hand while you're looking for the keys with the other hand.

Seeing you take part in this aerobic exercise, half of the kids get into the spirit of things and feel compelled to begin a vigorous game of, *Chinese Fire Drill*! The other half decides it's their turn to drive. Halfway through *Where-Are-the-Seat-Belts?!,* you notice the one-year-old has abandoned his car seat all together, and is missing in action. The five-year-old is running through the mud puddles in the front yard with his socks over his shoes, because you'd apparently told him to put on his "shoes and socks" not his "socks and shoes."

Once on the road and in-between "Stop hitting!" and "Sit back down!" you realize it will be a miracle if you don't get into a wreck. Also included on this joyride, is the insurmountable task of trying to sneak past all your children's favorite fast food restaurants, before they erupt into their uncontrollable, "Gotta have hamburgers and French fries" frenzies.

Just because you are all in the car doesn't mean the eating hours have stopped. No parent can withstand the overwhelming, engulfing pressure connected to the relentless demands emanating from this many kids. It's peer pressure in reverse. So, hamburgers and French fries it is. Yippee!

Arrival at the store is dissertation time. You go through your ritual, nose-to-nose. Your not-so-veiled death threats merely bounce off the kids like hot super balls. Had you somehow learned to speak in foreign tongues? Clawing and fighting their way out of the car, they zoom across the parking lot, and, like a swarm of hungry locusts, they jettison into the store. Along with the car, you sense the store is also trying *its* earnest best to hide.

Once inside, and to no avail, you desperately search for the shopping cart equipped with the "electric shock handcuffs." These handcuffs ground out whenever the child's other hand touches anything in the aisle. You quickly observe that your one-year-old wants absolutely nothing to do with the shopping cart seat, while your older ones fist-fight over being the one who gets to ride in it. Reiterating your earlier death threats, you quietly and calmly lead your little army of banditos through the store.

What may appear to many as a "calm and collected" parent at the store, is actually someone who still has just enough strength to suppress rage. We're not talking about the ability to suppress being "upset." We're talking about being able to suppress the wrath and fury only known by a nuclear weapon! Outwardly, that parent can appear to be the most calm and collected parent at the store. Inwardly, that parent is deranged and caffeine-deplet- ed— and either still has the strength to suppress this rage, or is in complete, catatonic apathy.

The kids are quick to learn that being in public "protects" them from your sincerest desires to vaporize them. By keeping the experience in a complete state of chaos, you'll actually forget who did what, thus enabling them to perform, and get away with, murder. This is called, "leverage." Unfortunately, this "leverage" always seems to be on the wrong side of the fulcrum.

Doubting if *Lloyds of London* would insure your family's trip to the store, you use the utmost care and caution as you weave your horde of renegades up and down the multi-thousand-dollar aisles of potential bankruptcy. Visions of milk mixed with kitty litter, pickles, and macaroni & cheese cascading through the aisles dance through your head, reminding you of your mission—GET IN AND OUT AS FAST AS POSSIBLE WITH THE LEAST AMOUNT OF DAMAGE!

In the instant it takes for you to reach up for the jar of peanut butter on the shelf, your five-year-old decides to take over the piloting of the shopping cart into any one of a 335,002 different directions. As a result of his driving skills, you always prepare yourself to confront anything from three sets of bruised shins, ankles, and knees, to a mop and bucket dangling from the fists of the irate store manager, who, unfortunately recognizes you from before...

Adding a little more spice to the family's shopping expedition, your three-year-old proudly announces, with reckless abandon, to every customer walking by that he has poop in his pants. Wonderful—a new aromatherapy. Meanwhile, your one-year-old decides he's displeased with what you've chosen for dinner and proceeds to empty the shopping cart all over the aisle.

After a half-hour of refereeing 47,002 different mind-boggling games of *Put-That-Back!* and *Don't-Touch-That!*, you slowly push your cart (*now overflowing with God knows what!*) toward the check-stands. Like a shark stalking its prey, you zero in on your helpless target, the cashier, who—you guessed it—is desperately trying her earnest best to hide. In fact, she's still in therapy from the last time you were there. This was when she had to babysit your kids for 20 minutes while you tore through the shopping bags trying to decide what should stay and what should go because you left your wallet at home and didn't have enough cash to pay the bill.

Realizing there's no way out, her left eye and elbow begin to twitch uncontrollably with every step you take toward her. She digs through her purse and pulls out a prescription bottle. Her twitch turns into jitters. Her jitters turn into trembles. Pills scatter all around her as her left eye begins to roll back into her head and saliva starts to foam from her mouth. She's having a full-fledged grand mal seizure, for God's sake! All she can do is helplessly grasp at the sides of the cash register as her knees begin to buckle out from under her. You sincerely want to help her but you're too busy having a complete heavyweight, knock-down, drag-out, bar-fight with your three-year-old because he's taken your wallet and won't give it back!

Your kid is getting the best of you, and since all your other kids are ransacking the mechanical toys anyway, you negotiate a trade—your wallet for a horsey ride. It works!

After a wave goodbye to the cashier (who's now being airlifted to the hospital, again) you add 10 more minutes to your shopping trip for the inevitable *Horsey-Ride-Fights* at the *Showdown at Gumball Corral*. The resin-eyed, money-eating machines—lined up like soldiers standing guard at the door—are designed to inhale all of your change as compensation for bringing the kids to store in the first place.

On your way to the machines, however, you suddenly notice the sweet aroma of your favorite espresso brewing from around the corner. "Mmmmm... coffee..." you say to yourself as you levitate and float in a dream-like hypnotic state toward the fragrant perfume of caffeine. The wisps of vapor from the nectar of the gods beckon to you, playfully tickling your nostrils.

Faint whispers slowly harmonize into angelic voices speaking directly to you. "Why, dear parent, you poor soul. Following such a disastrous shopping spree, you really deserve a little pleasure—the only pleasure of the day, quite frankly. Surely a little cup of coffee isn't going to hurt anybody, now is it? You really, *really* do deserve it."

Your dream-like trance soon turns into frenzied ambition! "Why yes! You are absolutely right. I do deserve a cup of coffee! After all, I am a grown human being! I am an adult, by golly! I have rights, you know! I *should* reward myself!" You concur.

All of the voices chant in angelic unison, "That's right! You can think for yourself now. Go and live life again, humble parent!"

So after juggling the baby, the groceries, and whatever's left of your change, you order a 20 oz. *Quadruple-Grande-Raspberry-Mocha-Cappuccino-Latte-with-Light-Ice-and-No-Whip*, as a special reward for what you have endured, and for the long, arduous ride home.

Leaving a trail of groceries, your screaming, wet and hungry one-year-old, and you in the dust, it's time for the older kids' mad, mad race back across the busy parking lot to the car to see who gets to sit in the front. If it's one of the times you didn't lock your keys in the car, you can go ahead and load everybody in and conclude your shopping trip with the perilous drive back home.

Guzzling down half your latte, you back your car full of screaming banshees out of the parking spot. Having enough caffeine in you to carry the car full of kids home, and a heartbeat that would kill a humming bird, you sit and wait—vibrating at 18 billion RPMs—for your turn to go. With your engine also revving at 18 billion RPMs, sweat oozing out of your temples, and a grip on the steering wheel so tight it would decapitate a rhinoceros, you creatively bullet your wagon of mayhem into the 0.00001 mph traffic.

Timing is everything. Your NASCAR move lands you smack dab behind a giant billboard-on-wheels, which is pumping exhaust directly up your wind-tunnel nostrils. The lane-changing, quick-in-the-turn, race-car-driver in you knows there's only one alternative–change lanes immediately!

Clutching the other half of your life-giving espresso, you flip on the turn signal–any turn signal–and prepare to merge into another lane (Merge: [murj] (v.) to combine, blend, or unite gradually). Yeah, right. Will anybody let you in? Oh, hell no! You don't exist! They're all tunnel-visioned on the car directly ahead of them. And HEAVEN FORBID if anyone should squeeze in front of them!

After 35 wild and anything-but-discreet attempts at this death-defying lane change, you close your eyes, crank the wheel, and away you go–slamming on your brakes immediately! Huh?! You're stuck in a bottleneck because some poor schmuck's car has overheated directly in front of you. Will anybody let you back into the lane you just left? Of course not. They OWN that piece of property now! You lost all your rights to it when you changed lanes a millisecond ago.

In your haste and madness to get back into your previous lane, you watch in slow motion, as what's left of your cup of heaven slips from your fingertips through the air, and bounces across the steering wheel, the gearshift, and your knee, to finally land sideways onto the floorboard! ARRGHHH!

To the avid espresso drinker, this is not a pretty sight. Watching the succulent, life-giving nectar gurgle out of the paper chalice onto such a greedy and unworthy filthy carpet is absolutely intolerable! Stopping a car full of screaming kids right in the middle of traffic to lick and steep and suck that latte out of the rug becomes your newest goal. Your *only* goal. (Not that anyone could actually become addicted that to that stuff, mind you. It's just that, well, you simply want your morning cup of coffee to ease you into the bright, new, cheery day—that's all.) And, you haven't even made it out of the */?!#*! parking lot yet!

Ah, so much for the euphoria of espresso. It's back to reality for you!

"Never have more children than you have car windows."

ERMA BOMBECK

12
HAPPY HOLIDAYS

'Twas three weeks before Christmas and all through the house;
The kids were decorating, including the mouse.
The tree had been toppled, at least three times thrice,
If it lasts until Christmas, that would be nice...
SHIRLEY WESTBROOK

While you'll definitely want to wrap all your screaming kids together in Christmas wrap and stamp their foreheads with Grandma's address, it's usually in your best interest not to do so. Grandparents aren't very receptive to that type of package showing up on their doorstep. It's better to cover your eyes, point at a name in the nearest Siberian phone book, and stamp *that* address on their foreheads—with no return address, of course.

Before you have kids, the word "holiday" represents "a festive and joyous time away from work." However, chasing umpteen kids every minute of every day, year in and year out will be your learning curve. Holidays will be anything but a "festive and joyous time!" You might as well bring Freddie Krueger back into the mix and let him take over!

"Holiday Season" begins every year with Halloween. And this

particular holiday never lasts just one night. It's the opening salvo for months of sugar-frenzied moments of hyper-kinetic non-reality. For days and weeks your kids will buzz around like exploding firecrackers left over from the 4th of July. You might stretch out the agony by trying to hide and ration their mountains of M&M's, Sugar Babies, caramel apples, popcorn balls, *ad infinitum*... However, hiding anything at all is like a GPS system giving off its own tracking signal announcing, "Here I am!" Or, you could let them eat every last piece of candy and junk food until they explode like microwaved goldfish—which is usually what happens, despite your watchdog efforts.

Either way, you're doomed to suffer through the tummy aches, toothaches, and headaches brought on by overdoses of sucrose, glucose, fructose, and dextrose. It's probably much easier to take the kids to the doctor once a year for an annual IV infusion of sugar rather than going through the paint-your-face and beg-for-candy ritual. Costs about the same too!

Just about the time the sugar fix starts to die down and the candy store bedrooms turn back into the kitchen/pantry, it's over the river and through the woods to Grandma and Grandpa's house for Thanksgiving Dinner you go!

Like any other outing, you dress the kids and dog up as nicely as possible, put the baby in his jungle gym car seat contraption and make your way out to the car. The car seat changes configuration every time you use it, so while refereeing the fight over who gets to sit in the front, you wrestle the baby and his car seat into the car. This is about the time you notice your little bundle of joy curiously looking up at you from his car seat as you bang and bump his head for the 463rd time on everything from the front bumper to the rear axle. You can't help but observe the child's utter dismay as he recites his own little prayer: **"God save me! Oh God. Please save me!"** In his wonderment, he can only question his family tree.

Right before you turn on the ignition, you give the screaming kids your usual "best behavior" speech followed by your usual authoritative bribes and death threats. The neighbors are lined up along the street to cheer you on as you pull away. Of course, all your bribes and threats sail straight out the window with the dog's water dish and your favorite sunglasses, but you've done your duty, and away you go!

When you arrive, you notice two of your kids running up to the front door without any coats and shoes. You are then informed by the most reliable sources (your other children who witnessed the event), that the coats and a pair-and-a-half of shoes are somewhere between 5th Avenue and the freeway entrance. The dog is wearing the other shoe.

As Grandma and Grandpa welcome you at their door, you'll never mistake that gleam in their not-so-innocent and not-so-affectionate eyes as "love!" It's actually a contrived look to hide their glee at seeing you on the receiving end after all those years of havoc you dragged them through—*The Universal Parent-Child Payback.*

However, something very interesting and mysterious occurs once you've entered their home. Almost surreal. You can never quite put your finger on it, but you think you've entered a euphoric fantasy-land of some sort. Following the typical, "It's so nice to see you..." and the, "My how you've grown..." pleasantries, the kids instantly and magically transform into responsible, intelligent, and inspiring adults. Even the wannabe-show-dog becomes civil and converses with charm and refinement.

You, on the other hand, aren't able to stop the rabid convulsions of vacillating deliriums and verbosities from spewing out your mouth! The only thing you can do is periodically slap the back of your head in the hopes of knocking enough sense into yourself to shut-the-heck-up! The only thing everyone else can do—including the dog—is to stare at you with genuine looks of sympathy and concern.

Even though Thanksgiving Dinner provides a cornucopia of ammunition to stockpile the kids' food fights for the remainder of the year, your kids sit down at the table and eat their entire meal with poise and clarity. They take turns speaking eloquently about their adventures at school. Eloquently? When did they learn to say anything other than, "I dunno?" It's so surreal you have to keep pinching your cheeks with the salad tongs while spasms of gibberish continue to dribble from your quivering lips.

They don't stop! The wannabe-show-dog is in on it too! He

sits quietly, patiently, and respectfully at the table, covertly peering at you over his hot cup of cider with his sly *"Got ya!"* look. He even adds to the conversation with an occasional comment or two when appropriate. You are dumbfounded! You can only succumb deeper and deeper into your pathetic state of babbling neurosis.

After what seems like an eternity, Grandma finally lets you know it's time to go and makes sure you have enough fruitcake and pumpkin pie to take with you. So, with a heartfelt, "It's been nice to see you..." and a, "Happy Thanksgiving..." she zealously hands the kids and the dog their pre-Christmas stockings full of candy, cookies, and little toys. The kids and the dog give their wonderful grandparents hugs and kisses, and out the door to the car you all go!

.00000000000000000000000000000000001 milliseconds after the last wave goodbye can be waved, it happens!

> *There are arms and legs and bubble gum trees!*
> *There are antlers, fan belts and fruitcakes too!*
> *You have screaming gazelles, luminous fish and honeybees!*
> *And tubas and scubas and chimpanzees too!*

MAYHEM! The kids are screaming eight octaves above high C! And all sugared up for the-month-before-Christmas! Yay!!

Christmas shopping is that joyous time of year for exchanging greetings and expressive hand gestures while torpedoing the car full of screaming, cold, tired, and hungry kids through miles of icy gridlocked traffic. These traffic jams consist of other cars full of screaming, cold, tired, and hungry kids being driven by screaming, cold, tired, and caffeinated adults who have about as much patience as a swarm of frozen hornets on fire! Racing through the maze of cars to find a parking spot can only be accomplished with the grace and finesse of a Kamikaze jet fighter with NASCAR moves.

Adding to the treacherousness of finding a place to park, Christmas shopping becomes a free-for-all of sugared-up kids bouncing up and down store aisles, potty breaks, and double-checking your life insurance policy. By the time you get through the mangled aisles of broken toys, head counts, and harried cashiers, the mad race is on to wait in the 75-minute line to sit on Santa's lap.

Seeing Santa is the highlight of your Christmas shopping excursion. Once the kids are old enough to understand who Santa is, and can verbalize what they want for Christmas, there is simply no stopping them. They will proceed to give Santa the exact, precise, literal, particular, clear-cut, defined, detailed specifics of their little hearts' desires.

And, there is no stopping Santa from promising them that they WILL get "from Santa" that brand-new, multimillion dollar, X-19 turbo-injected, freewheeling, computerized, anti-gravity, laser-guided, hydrogen-propelled, 14K gold-plated, diamond-studded, fur-lined, thermonuclear, biochemical, insect-repelling, waterproof, shock-resistant, heavy duty, lightweight, compact, one-of-a-kind, time traveling, ninja, quick release, antimissile, hyper speed, one-size-fits-most, mind reading, budget planning, logarithmic, light-censored, tuna fishing, NASA approved, can't-live-without, disposable, stealth-detecting, fully armed, sugar-free, radar jamming, storm trooping, assembly required, biodegradable, hand-held, bulletproof, toilet-trained, odorless, transforming, fourth dimension toy that's been advertised EVERY minute of EVERY day in EVERY newspaper and

EVERY magazine and on EVERY TV and EVERY radio station on planet Earth for the past 11 months and costs about as much as USA's Gross National Debt!

During the ride home, you desperately try to come up with excuses as to why "Santa" may not be able to come through with "his" promise of delivering the brand-new, multimillion dollar, X-19 turbo-injected, freewheeling, computerized, anti-gravity, laser-guided, hydrogen-propelled, 14K gold-plated, diamond-studded, fur-lined, thermonuclear, biochemical, insect-repelling, waterproof, shock-resistant, heavy duty, lightweight, compact, one-of-a-kind, time traveling, ninja, quick release, antimissile, hyper speed, one-size-fits-most, mind reading, budget planning, logarithmic, light-censored, tuna fishing, NASA approved, can't-live-without, disposable, stealth-detecting, fully armed, sugar-free, radar jamming, storm trooping, assembly required, biodegradable, hand-held, bulletproof, toilet-trained, odorless, transforming, fourth dimension whatchamacallit.

Once home, this one-of-a-kind adventure has you dropping to your knees in complete exhaustion in your personal haven, the *Twiddly-Lips* corner. The twitching in your right eye and the drool from the corner of your mouth forges a new-found sympathy for that cashier at the grocery store.

Along with Christmas shopping comes the next big thing... yay! You got it—DeCoRaTiNg! Like most responsible parents, you carefully hide the decorations in the attic. Like most responsible parents, you also forget your little band of constructors had built forts in the attic all summer long and had unearthed the Christmas decorations long ago. You'll know when it's time to decorate because your ridiculously overzealous little *Frank Lloyd Wrights* have strewn

Christmas lights, angel hair, and tinsel throughout each and every bedroom, bathroom, and closet!

And then comes the day of your boss's annual Christmas party. The boss's annual Christmas party is always one of those anxiety-filled, no-getting-out-of events. You find an unsuspecting babysitter, brief her on how to handle sugared-up, hyped-up, innovative, Christmas-is-coming, miniature 007's, and give her the telephone numbers of three backup sitters "just in case."

From all the stress—as well as your own intake of too much sugar, you might find this to be a perfect time to grow a pimple on your nose. Not just any pimple. As you ready yourself for the party, without missing a beat and right in front of your eyes, this little red spot on your nose turns into the Mt. Vesuvius of all pimples! It's like watching Pinocchio watching his nose grow after telling one lie after another. Flash-forward 1,600 lies in 10 minutes. The pimple on your nose is so big that:

Santa wants YOU to guide his sleigh tonight.

It competes with Old Faithful during tourist season.

It's mistaken for Mt. Rushmore, because one can identify all of the Presidents' faces on it.

Tickets are being sold across America in anticipation of the impending eruption.

A single picture of it can only be taken from outside the solar system.

It announces you as its "tag-along" and proceeds to act as your emcee for the rest of the evening.

All the above.

Yay.

The party is a mix of young people, old people, single people, and mentally-deranged parents set free for an evening with other mentally-deranged parents—who are so far gone they can't complete a sentence anymore, let alone hold an intelligent conversation if they tried. And, of course, there is your boss's wife who is only let out once a year for this glorious event. They also have boys—five.

At last year's party, she had been so happy to escape the mantle of parenthood for three hours, that she had a little more "cheer" than she was used to and proceeded to give table dances for all the guests while spitting and slobbering out one of the sloppiest renditions of, *Take This Job and Shove It* anyone would not want to hear—all the while dressed and wrapped in what was left of the Christmas tree! (She felt the shiny star on top and tinsel made for a great costume.) Ah, the joys of parenthood.

Realizations start to creep in and build. This poor mother is only one step ahead of you. Is this your future? Your fate? Christmas spent wrapped in tree decorations singing *Take This Job and Shove It*? Your pimple grows another foot—it can now officially stand on its own.

Your wonderful evening with people who can no longer complete sentences and the other people who intelligently ignore you is interrupted and ended by frantic phone calls from the *number two* backup babysitter. She's wondering if you know where the other backup babysitters are—and if it's okay for her to have friends over to "help" (*eat you out of house and home*). You politely say good night to the other deranged parents, who give you an all-knowing haunted look (because they overheard your end of the phone calls), and you and "Old Faithful" say your good-byes and go home.

On Christmas morning, you awaken to a panorama of children joyously frolicking through mountains of wrapping paper stuck to owner's manuals belonging to scattered, half-assembled toys.

Your wannabe-show-dog and the neighbor's cat are happily lapping up spilled juice, coffee, and eggnog while the kids devour the contents of their Christmas stockings full of Grandma's cookies and candy. Even though the 10-pound box of chocolates is empty and every candy cane in the neighborhood has been consumed, the kids and dog and cat are all still hungry.

The blur of *Christmas Sugarland* leads you nicely into New Year's Eve. New Year's touches on somewhat of a delicate subject because of the enormous emphasis placed on drinking alcohol. The adult who is not a parent is free to party, frolic, and dance to their heart's content. They can wake up the next morning whenever they choose and glide gently into New Year's Day without a hitch.

However, the mere thought of waking up to a mind-bending, room-whirling, excruciatingly blinding, too-sick-to-puke, out-of-aspirin hangover coupled with the parental responsibilities of chasing down and changing wet, poopy diapers, while simultaneously catering to a morning rush of the loudest, most demanding and inconsiderate, screaming, hungry kids is NOT something many humans can tolerate! Did I mention "loud"? Unless you're into pain, you can count *out* New Year's Eve.

And then, just about the time you get all of the tinsel vacuumed up, along comes the Easter grass. Oh goody.

"If you want to see what children can do, you must stop giving them things."

NORMAN DOUGLAS

"Train up a child in the way he should go: and when he is old, he will not depart from it."

PROVERBS 22:6
KING JAMES VERSION

13

OFF TO SCHOOL

Like most parents, you excitedly, exuberantly, and ecstatically look forward to when your kids are old enough to go to school. You joyfully send your little "geniuses-to-be" off to learn what you fondly remember as "reading, writing, and arithmetic."

However, and almost immediately, mixed in with their cute little pictures of colorful, round, triangular squares, they bring home that dreaded anathema: homework! Before long, their homework starts to resemble volumes of hieroglyphic equations equating to the amount of information found only in the Library of Congress! Like you really have time for that...

Being the "geniuses-to-be," your children quickly learn that along with report cards, homework is something to be hidden from ALL adults at ALL times, and under absolutely NO circumstances is it EVER to be completed. They aren't there to learn anything except the graces of social status anyway. After all, that's what school is for, right?

After a brief reprieve in your day, your *Super Parent Sixth Sense* starts to go on high alert as the three o'clock hour–school dismissal–approaches. Preparing for this daily ritual, you mentally and physically barricade yourself away from the front door and seek refuge in your *Twiddly-Lips* corner. Feeling as though you're about to face a firing squad, you reluctantly go ahead and ask the question every parent dreads, but has to ask, "Do you have any homework?"

Your feeble gesture quickly fades into a whirlwind of fliers, special notes, and books (all in triplicate), scattered throughout the living room, dining room, and kitchen. When the dust finally settles, you slowly open your eyes and focus in on what you so fondly remembered as being your beloved refrigerator. Its contents are strewn over all of the counters, across the kitchen floor, and through the back door (which is dangling from one of its hinges), and then over the fence to the neighbor's back yard! And your oldest child isn't even out of the second grade yet!

Before you know it, the inevitable happens—*Parent-Teacher Conferences*. Initially the conferences start with a note or a call from the teacher expressing his or her interest in the progress of your child. Sounds innocent enough, right? Nope. Not really.

On the way to your initial face-to-face meeting with the dreaded teacher (i.e., judge, jury, prosecutor, executioner...), a record-breaking case of AAD ("Anticipatory-Anxiety Disorder") kicks in, due to your much anticipated PTD ("Parent-Teacher Disorder"). Even though you only suspect what may come up in the meeting, it's all you can do to psych yourself out with rehearsed excuses explaining your child's inattentiveness in class. The teacher's curiosity about the parent of their "most interesting pupil" puts you under the searing microscope of "worthy parent" examination even more.

Your rehearsed excuses give way to caffeine-induced mumblings of lamebrain sob stories as to why your little Johnny has been behind in his homework. The fact that you can't stop this gambit of excuses and promises to do better from spewing out of your mouth only serves to confirm the teacher's suspicions as to why your little Johnny is, in fact, behind in his schoolwork.

The conferences always end with your assurances to help your child with his homework. This includes, but is not limited to, memorizing all of the axioms and geochemical formulas related to the hypotenuse of an isosceles triangle while at the same time writing a complete dissertation on how it all relates *specifically* to the reasons why he likes football. The extra credit bonus is based on learning all of the relationships between the seen and unseen particles, waves, and strings streaming between Earth and Alpha Centauri. You are now going to have to learn everything you missed in second grade! Yippee!

Another side effect of helping your seven-year-old with his Thesis Statement, entitled *Formation of Pantheistic Geometrical Trigonometry*, is the mind-blowing realization that if you're ever going to escape the financial duress that comes with parenting, you might have to commit yourself to a classroom as well.

If you do make the decision to advance your own education, the first thing that happens is you'll enroll too late to find classes geared toward your major–*Resignation Letter Writing*. As a result, you will find yourself marooned in the only remaining elective–*Philosophy of Religion and Physics*, with beady-eyed Professor Sigmund Whampt De Whumpf.

Your first homework assignment will be writing a six-and-a-half-pound tome on the distinct relationship between the "Big Bang Mechanics of Three-Dimensional Time vs. Space Ratios Inside Cygnus X-1," and "Theology—As It Is/Was/Will Be Two Time Streams to the Left." Unfortunately, your homework assignment will be vacuumed up by the bending of time and space you have to do in order to make dinner for your vortex of genetically confused barbarians!

Some patterns never change. You'll allow yourself the freedom of putting off your homework until the very last millisecond. Right? Your grades will simply reflect how much talent you have in gaining sympathy by advancing your pathetic sob stories and excuses.

Unfortunately, you learn right off the bat, the Honorable Mr., Dr., no-nonsense, beady-eyed, Professor Sigmund Whampt De Whumpf doesn't care if the kids used the garden hose to fill up your gas tank, or if the dog got the next-door neighbor's cat pregnant... You're in for your own personal *Parent-Teacher Conference!* Yay! And, oh yeah, he wants your parents' phone number too.

So much for your escape through education. Now it's back to the kids!

Extracurricular activities (such as homework) are not your only nemeses. Throw in the kids' last minute surprise of field trips, picture days, more calls from teachers, detentions... and the typical school week is complete.

With regards to field trips, you're usually reminded to have a lunch consisting of a sandwich, some type of fruit, a snack, and something to drink in a non-breakable container—just as the school bus is pulling up.

Wearing your bathrobe and a younger sibling or two wrapped around your leg, you rush out the door with a bagged lunch in hand, greet your neighbors, sprint halfway down the street, shove

the lunch through the bus window, and wave goodbye to your little pioneer! The neighbors place bets to see if you make it to the bus on time. It becomes a spectator event.

Regarding class pictures, learning about picture day is almost as exciting as learning about field trips. Depending on the particular year, you'll find out about Picture Day just as the bus is pulling up, or a month later, when your children bring home $3,000 worth of invoices for an assortment of 900,000 useless wallet-size pictures so you can get the free bonus 8x10.

Of course, these pictures are usually taken the day after Halloween. This is when half the kids' costume makeup is still on, and when they have solidified chocolate smeared up and down the front of their shirts. Their hair is still sticking up from the gum they forgot to take out of their mouths before going to bed. It's too late for retakes, so all your relatives are simply stuck with pictures documenting the new hairdo trends created by your hip and innovative kids.

Having pictures taken at a professional studio is another event that requires an attempt to get your kids to look good. "Look your best" becomes a relative term. The battle of keeping the kids clean is on! Using the universal cleaning tools for all parents (tissue and spit), you try to clean the chocolate off of them from that one melted candy bar they always find stuck between the car seats just as you're pulling into the portrait studio's parking lot.

You start the "sitting" by chasing your horde of renegades around and through the photographer's 1,000 miles of electrical spaghetti which is connected to absurdly expensive-looking equipment strategically laid out across even more absurdly expensive-looking equipment.

After untangling yourself and your one-year-old's poopy, wet diaper from the latest version of the photographer's "1600 LED CN2x-180 Ultra High Power Dimmable Panel Analog Digital" camera's tripod, it's time to get all of your kids and the dog to sit still long enough for the F-Stop to capture them.

If you get that far, choosing the family portrait becomes your next incomprehensible chore. It's rare to get a family portrait where all of the kids are smiling and facing in the same direction—preferably *toward* the camera—*and* at the same time. You'll throw out the pictures where baby is teething on the electric cords and settle on any picture that didn't expose more than one child picking his or anyone else's nose.

And speaking of body parts...

14

THE DOCTOR'S OFFICE

If you end up with several rambunctious kids, chances are you'll become well acquainted with the doctor's office and emergency room. The ER may even have a padded room with a revolving door reserved just for you.

When stranded for hours on end in a waiting room, reality as you know it will no longer exist. It's like being lost in an adjacent dimension or two where, apparently, there is no concept of time as you remember it. You're caught in an alien reality. *Your* time is the doctor's LAST concern in the whole wide world. And why not? They have a monopoly on it! After all, *their* time is *your* money. So you have no choice but to wait, and wait, and wait some more in—you guessed it—the WAITING room!

You'll wait, all right! In fact, you'll wait so long you have enough time to read every *National Geographic* ever published from cover to cover and still have enough time to find all of the objects in the Hidden Pictures™ Puzzles in every *Highlights* magazine ever printed! You'll also referee 3,649 Olympic-style *He-Hit-Me-First* games concurrently being held in each and every hallway, corridor, and elevator of the hospital by your other not-so-sick children. One of the kids may even graduate high school while you're waiting!

The correct term for the waiting room is, *"Asylum for Caffeine-Depleted Parents."* You will even stoop so low as to drink coffee from the vending machine. Waiting with a sick child requires the mental and physical prowess of a cross-eyed elephant frolicking through a peanut farm. However, waiting with a sick child while corralling three, or four, or five rambunctious healthy children mixed with visions of being quarantined forever due to an Ebola outbreak, requires the supernatural powers of an ascended master!

It's the usual waiting room worries. Will your kid be OK? Are you going to be leaving with the same number of kids you started out with? Is the dog going to hot-wire the car so he can go joy riding and chase stray cats—again?

When the nurse finally comes out and says the doctor is ready to see you, don't mistake this encouraging announcement for the truth. After you round up your herd of wild banditos and slowly make your way around and through all the other sniveling parents with their whining kids to your specially-padded examining room, you'll be told to wait some more. This is a shorter wait though. There's only enough time to referee 32 football games with the stethoscopes, rubber gloves, and tourniquets the kids found hiding in the cupboards!

By then, your "sick" child has all of a sudden become well enough to join the other kids frolicking, leaping, and bouncing their way around the room like a pack of polka-dotted gazelles. They'll be jumping around so much you forget which child is supposed to be sick.

Of course, this is just in time for the doctor to buzz into the examination room. While dodging scissors, stethoscopes, and flying syringes spinning and darting across his forehead, he asks, "What seems to be the problem?"

"I think it's this one," you respond as you peel your little jumping bean off the ceiling, while also disentangling another child out from under the examining table.

Upon a quick check, the doctor pulls a BB out of the kid's ear, and away you go! Just in time, too.

After finally untangling yourself from 600 feet of bandages, gauze, and tape, you can hear the car horn in the distance. Your wannabe-*Chauffeur*-dog has grown impatient.

So, it's back home you go with a new and improved fixed kid! Yahoo.

"The tooth fairy teaches children that they can sell body parts for money."

DAVID RICHERBY

"The reason grandparents and grandchildren get along so well is that they have a common enemy."

SAM LEVENSON

15

BABYSITTER WANTED

Finding a reliable babysitter has its challenges—particularly if you're a long-haired musician, single dad with four rambunctious and inventive boys who also come with a red-haired, greyhound-looking, wannabe-show-dog. As with any parent, especially a single parent, there are more than just a few death-defying mental and physical hoops to jump through when you're in need of a babysitter.

In my case, there were band rehearsals to attend. A typical rehearsal consisted of several trips to the diaper bag, refilling baby bottles with whatever was closest at hand, and regularly extracting gum from my four-year-old's hair—not to mention also having to constantly throw bath toys at them as a backup plan to get them to stop doing whatever it was they weren't supposed to be doing. All the while, yours truly is catching the three-year-old as he played *Leap from a Chair to Swing on Dad's Guitar Neck* in the middle of every chorus.

Giving the band my "kids will be kids" look and telling them, "All is well..." had about as much effect as corralling a herd of stampeding rhinoceroses with an ostrich feather. The band was either going to move on without me, or I'd have to do the impossible—find a babysitter.

In most cases, looking for babysitters was like lighting up a billboard in the sky with a super magnet announcing, **"Single Parent Musician Taking Applications From Untamed-Crazy-Psycho-Groupies ONLY!"**

Musicians attract the most incredible array of babysitting talent you could *NOT* want to imagine. The saying, "Scraping the bottom of the barrel" doesn't even apply here. There's no barrel to scrape. I spent the majority of my time interviewing, hiring, and then losing several different babysitters. For me, the "babysitting hiring pool" consisted primarily of flirtatious, pregnant 16-year-olds; blind 75-year-old grandmas; or 32-year-old "drill sergeants." They all had their own agendas, which had very little to do with taking care of my kids.

Most sitters came with problems. For example, I had to replace one sitter because I started receiving 2 a.m. phone calls from prisoners who were being released from the county jail, looking for a "good time." Apparently, the sitter's name and my phone number were etched into the cement wall next to the pay phone at the prisoner's exit. Adios sitter! Hello panic! The frantic search was on again. Too bad too, because she was really good with the kids.

Desperation rushed in. I needed a sitter. And I needed one quick! So, I did what most parents do—put out a 911 to all of my friends for help. Since they all knew my situation, there wasn't a chance on this side of the moon they'd volunteer to babysit—but, they would help me *find* a babysitter. If they were the other band members, they would go out of their way to ask all of their friends and anyone else they met in their daily journeys.

In my case, a manager at the local grocery store heard of my plight. She had seen our family before, but because she had never experienced the complete package first-hand, she offered to help me out. Since she was a store manager *and* a mom, "responsibility" was the only word about her that penetrated what was left of my Swiss-cheesed, worry-riddled mind. Finally, someone who understood the challenges of parenthood!

The very next night, I introduced the kids to the new babysitter. She was authoritative, yet caring. Without breaking stride, she immediately asked each child what their favorite game was and began running the household with complete confidence and excitement.

She shooed me out because I was in her way, reassuring this overly anxious, mentally-deranged, single parent musician dad, "All is well... The kids and I will be just fine. So off to work you go!"

"Thank you, God. Thank you!" I said to myself as tears of gratitude started to tremble down my face. "There's hope now. Everything will be okay... Thank you! Thank you! Thank you!" And off I went!

When I arrived at the gig, the other band members greeted me with great relief. They had been concerned I wouldn't make it—and rightly so. There's nothing like trying to play a gig without a band member.

After playing the first set I called home anxiously. The babysitter calmly and cheerfully said the kids were all fed, in bed and everything was fine. She insisted I stop worrying and stop calling or I'd wake them up. Awesome! "Thank you, God! Thank you!" I exclaimed in ecstatic relief!

After playing a couple more sets with no frantic phone call interruptions, I began to relax. After all, a responsible parent was watching my kids and all was well. This sense of well-being seeped into my soul. What a relief. My new babysitter was a godsend.

So why should I have been the least bit concerned when she showed up (75 miles away from home) during the last set of my gig dressed in white go-go boots, a black leather mini-skirt, and a pink blouse tied up to her cleavage? Why should the fact that she was wielding enough lipstick, eye shadow, and hairspray to build a client list stretching from Amsterdam to Bangkok to Hollywood and back again bother me? From my vantage point on stage, this was not looking good.

The show must go on. As I played, she teased. She teased every single (and not-so-single) guy from one end of the beer-soaked dance floor to the other! No one was safe from her affectionate and slithering pole dance moves. The fact that she disappeared with the local softball team during the last 20 minutes of the set shouldn't have bothered me either, right?

And for heaven's sake, why should I have been the least bit concerned when my godsend of a babysitter finally made it back to the club just in the nick of time for a ride home? After all, I hired a responsible mom and trustworthy store manager, right?

Just because her makeup was smeared from ear-to-ear, her blouse was completely mis-buttoned, her skirt was on sideways shouldn't have worried me either, right? Not to mention the fact she had also developed a rapid-fire speech impediment! None of this should have caught my attention either, right? All was well?

Of course, this comedy of errors didn't end there. It had to be followed up with a mentally-grueling, cigarette smoke-filled, hour-and-a-half ride home. This ride consisted of some of the wildest sexual overtures anyone would *NOT* want to experience—well, while driving anyway—mixed with an impromptu job interview for advancing her career by supporting my musical endeavors as my new "business manager." She had obviously proven the worth of her responsibility and personal managing skills by taking the liberty of hiring a "live-in" sitter to watch my kids so she could be at all of my gigs to "cheer me on" (including the one I just played). Huh? I'd hired a store-manager/call-girl/business-manager?

As I pulled into my moonlit driveway, I noticed a pair of muddy, size 13 Sasquatch footprints walking up the side of my house to my oldest son's first floor bedroom. Being the simple, run-of-the-mill, long-haired musician, single father that I was, I should have welcomed this unusual turn of events and simply went on, right?

I was told by my new live-in sitter—a seven-month pregnant, 15-year-old runaway—that the trail of muddy footprints going up one side of my house and down the other belonged to her 18-year-old boyfriend. Ah, at least I didn't have to worry about Bigfoot anymore. This shouldn't have been much of a surprise either, right? As it turned out, Mr. Romeo Sasquatch Bigfoot had been up to a little mischief himself and was apparently wanted by the FBI for armed robbery and assault. He had reasoned that climbing through the front window was more "discreet" than coming in through the front door. How thoughtful.

Could it get any better? Let's see... I had a mentally-grueling, cigarette smoke-filled, hour-and-a-half ride with the babysitter, met my new live-in seven-month pregnant, 15-year-old runaway sitter, and scared away an 18-year-old fugitive wanted by the FBI and probably a half-dozen other government agencies.

What happened with the men/women in blue, you may wonder? Oh, they showed up, gripping the arms of the original sitter's rain-soaked, mentally-crazed, and not-so-ex-husband. He was caught stalking my house looking for his babysitter/store-manager/call girl/business manager/wife. So much for, "All was well..."

I know these wild and crazy babysitter experiences might sound a little extreme, but hey, I'm a musician. Right? Oh well. Back to the drawing board!

As a working single parent, having a "live-in" sitter not only makes sense, it may very well be a necessity. However, it's extremely difficult when your finances dictate that the choices of babysitters only come from the bottom of the hiring pool. Most of the babysitters need you to babysit them just as much as you need them to babysit your kids. Your choices, unfortunately, are either nomads looking for a place to live, or teenagers needing a place to hide—neither of which want anything to do with you or your kids.

Their workday goes like this: you leave; they lie on the couch—their oasis. One minute before you return, and during that one minute, they'll attempt to clean, cook, and change a day's or night's worth of wet, poopy diapers before you enter the door. You look to the dog for his employment application, but he refuses the job.

Your rambunctious boys intuitively sense, and thus seize, any lazy babysitter opportunity. They will wait for the babysitter to fall asleep on the couch and then conduct their scientific experiments. This includes, but is not limited to, pouring buckets of milk, car oil, and dish water all over the living room carpet and hardwood floors. Oh, those unanticipated expenses of raising children—but that's another chapter.

After a vigorous *Carpet-Ripping Party-of-One*, along with

your usual, *Pulling-Your-Hair-Out-Tantrum*, you sop up the mess by using every towel, blanket, and innocent by-standing cat you can find hiding around the house to use as sponges. Once that's accomplished, you can then go ahead and shove a couple sizzling hot electrical portable heaters under the sopping wet carpet. Of course, three days later there's a new scientific experiment and the entire process repeats itself. Solution: find a new babysitter.

At first, you'll think of the usual options for babysitters: grandparents and great-grandparents. However, you'll have no choice but to eliminate the poor, frail elderly from the onset. First of all, they think they have been reduced to the condition of "has-been" humans and are simply not qualified for that type of work any-

more. They've had quite enough already, thank you! Second of all, your kids may not appreciate being hunted down and smothered with sloppy Polident-filled kisses by what *they* see as, "shriveled, one-eyed, toothless, prune-faced, deaf hags and geezers who are chasing their septic, dilapidated false teeth around their faces with their glutinous, decomposing tongues!"

The greatest of grandmas and grandpas simply meander through life in a foggy state of amnesia, with silly little pleasantries and religious affirmations drooling from their quivering lips. It's all they can do to spend their waking days pushing their walkers from one end of their bedroom to the other. This is not to mention constantly being followed around the house with a handful of baby-wipes and a pooper-scooper because of the half-filled adult diapers dangling between *their* legs!

The sad fact is, they'll never see the light of consciousness as they once knew it ever again. So on to more applicable prospects we go!

While interviewing potential live-in sitters, you learn to pinpoint exactly what's required. You have to be very specific. You're not looking for a wife, husband, fiancé, boyfriend, or girlfriend. And you really don't want or desire a babysitter/cashier/call-girl/business manager/groupie either. You simply need a dependable, accountable, responsible person to watch your kids. Is that asking too much? Uh, oh yeah, and for free?

During the interview process for a live-in sitter, you can use the following criteria:

- Do they have a pulse? (Having a pulse is a very good sign.)
- Does their blood contain any human DNA? (You'd be surprised.)

- Can they point? (In any direction?)
- Do they have references? (Preferably people to whom they don't owe money.)
- Will they let go of a cookie to free their hand from a jar? (Well… Will they?)
- Can they drive a car without killing every living thing between the driveway and the grocery store?
- Can they cook—anything? (Anything at all?)
- Can they read—anything? (Anything at all?)
- How is their personal hygiene? (Can you get close enough to find out?)
- Can they operate a telephone?
- Can they tell the difference between "911" (nine-eleven) and "9+1+1" (nine-one-one)? (I wish I was exaggerating.)

It's a numbers game. There will be a couple of times when you get lucky. Believe it or not, there are some innocent souls who start out as *Good Samaritans* and come to your rescue. When this happens, you'll definitely learn to be welcoming and courteous during these seemingly once-in-a-lifetime opportunities.

Having someone over the age of six who's willing to converse intelligently with you means an awful lot. Even though you're no longer capable of engaging in these types of conversations, the movement of their lips, their facial expressions, and peculiar sounds are most pleasing and amusing to you.

The fact that you act like a completely-starved-for-affection recluse who's been stranded on a deserted island for three-and-a-half years never enters your godforsaken bewildered mind either.

You instinctively and unconsciously do anything and everything possible to make your new friend feel right at home.

This includes, but is not limited to, convulsively dropping to your wretched, bruised, and worn-out knees, hysterically kissing their hands and feet, while thanking them profusely every single time they enter or leave the living room. With your arms coiled tightly around their ankles as they drag you across the floor in an attempt to get away, you beg and cry in complete hysteria, "I'll do anything! I'll clean!! I'll cook!! I'll do all the chores! Please stay! Oh God! Just please, will you stay?!"

Uh, yeah… not exactly a good sitter-retention tactic. Oh well. Life goes on!

"I take a very practical view of raising children. I put a sign in each of their rooms: Checkout Time is 18 years."

ERMA BOMBECK

"A good film is when the price of the dinner, the theatre admission and the babysitter were worth it."

ALFRED HITCHCOCK

"Nothing has a stronger influence psychologically on their environment and especially on their children than the unlived life of the parent."

16
THE LOVE LIFE OF A SINGLE PARENT MUSICIAN

Really?

"I'm dating a woman now who, evidently, is unaware of it."

GARRY SHANDLING

17

DATE NIGHT

If you're a single parent musician like me, nothing will happen in a direct, simple manner. In my case, serendipity always took the upper hand and started the ball rolling in the most circuitous ways. To illustrate just how far off track and self-debasing a mentally-deficient single parent dad can get, I'll share my own personal dating story. Because this is very personal and somewhat embarrassing, please don't tell anybody.

Like most eight- and nine-year-olds, my kids were extremely innovative and artistic. They explored many expressions of art and became very acquainted with the many uses of scissors—especially with each other's hair. They invented hairdos as wild and creative as any makeup artist in the Hollywood horror film industry. As a result, one of their teachers informed me my kids needed real haircuts and gave me the number of a mom she knew who cut hair. So I called her, and made an appointment for the following Saturday morning.

This adventure started out just like the rest. Pack all the kids into my smoke-billowing 1972 Grand Torino Station Wagon and embark on a very uncertain and questionable drive to somewhere. Pulling up to our destination, I delivered an extra-special and long-winded, "Be On Your Best Behavior" dissertation. We got out of the car, walked up to the door, and knocked.

Corralling the kids onto the porch, I gave a recap of my, "Best Behavior" speech and gave a polite second knock on the door. It opened. To my complete and utter shock and awe, standing before me, was the most beautiful creature... no, angel... no, GODDESS I had EVER seen! She was surrounded by a brilliant halo of white golden light!

Her angelic glow and immortal essence saturated and penetrated through every fiber of my completely-deranged, been-with-kids-too-long, captured soul. It was all I could do to close my gaping mouth and keep from throwing myself on the ground in complete, humble, supplicating submission! I. Was. Spell. Bound.

Conversation? What conversation? I had been living in a vortex with my kids far too long to know what to say to a true-to-life goddess. My tongue began to swell three times its original size as my heart cartwheeled up and down my throat like a trampoline full of frogs chasing flies. As I clumsily stuttered through the usual pleasantries and, "How do you do's," the only conversation I could hear was a very blurred argument in my brain between Goofy, Gollum, and Yoda. They kept debating about which one of them she would go for first. The only one I was trying to listen to was Yoda, but he bailed!

Through all of this entangled mental mayhem, I could see, however, that my tongue-twisted gestures and hectic ramblings were of no consequence to her. She had the pure and elegant radiance of an angel, blanketing me with the merciful understanding and kindness of a saint. She was completely unscathed by my display of catatonic spasms and bewildered babble. After all, this scenario happened to her at least 1,752 times a day. Obviously.

After what seemed like an eternity, I finally got control of my kaleidoscope mind and gained enough common sense to let the kids do all my talking for me. Her grace even showered over them so they had no choice but to act like civil little grown-ups.

When she was finished cutting their hair, the kids were all very happy and pleased with the great job she did. How the heck did she do that? They turned into adults! They graciously thanked her with hugs and waves before skipping down the sidewalk and jumping into our 1972 Grand Torino Station Wagon. Tripping and stumbling, I contorted myself back to the car. I just couldn't take my eyes off of her angelic smile and sparkling eyes.

I was 16 again, and completely filled with a love beyond comparison. I could only reason that I was either having another out-of-body experience, or aliens had taken over and transported me to their homeland again. Haircuts? What haircuts? I didn't know what was happening. My mind and heart short-circuited into wild, passionate, infatuation. I felt the sting of Cupid's Arrow and possessed the Secret of the Sorcerer's Stone! I had just been blessed by the Grace of the Divine to meet such a glorious beam of encompassing light.

For the next two years, I lay awake every night wondering if I'd ever talk to her again. I looked for her at the gigs I was playing, on every street I walked, and whenever I had to take a kid to the emergency room. After all, she was a single mother of three young kids herself. Nothing, nothing, nothing. It really had been a once-in-a-lifetime chance meeting on the soul plane, which I couldn't even attempt to explain. I'd have to go to another dimension to find her again. Yep. That's where goddesses are found.

Fantasies of her being romantically involved with me—a single parent musician dad of four boys plus a wannabe-show-dog—flew directly in the face of picturing her laughing hysterically at such a ridiculous notion. This dilemma bounced back and forth in my mind like a ping-pong ball in a never-ending World Table Tennis Championship Tournament! I couldn't afford her financially or emotionally, yet I couldn't afford being without her either. What would happen if I really ever had the chance to speak to her again?

My mind froze. Talk to her? Talk to a goddess? Every time I looked into the mirror, I saw *Quasimodo* from the *Hunchback of Notre Dame* looking back at me. With sweaty palms and reverent care, I would pick up the phone and imagine calling her just in the hopes of hearing her enchanting voice. About 10 seconds later I'd put the phone down again. I did that 732.18 times. This was far worse than being 16.

I was completely out of control and desperate. Everyone in the household was miserable. Even my live-in sitter couldn't take it anymore. She finally delivered the ultimatum: "Either make the call or one of us is going to have to shoot ourselves."

Knowing I couldn't go on this way, I finally built up enough courage and took the leap of all leaps. I braced myself for the all-fatal and anticipated, *"No way! Are you kidding?!"* Click! And then I called the most beautiful creature I'd ever met. It went like this:

Her: "Hello?" (*Angelic Ambiance*)

Me: "Gfsretdbfatejngfhcfxbdbfergb?" (*Esoteric Hebrew/ Swahili/Gaelic/Pig Latin*)

Her: "Yes. I would be happy to. What did you have in mind?"

Me: "DgstBrhfb*dmDshhfb%njc)dn?"

Her: "Yes, I like comedy!"

Me: "Rfatemm$%ljhs?"

Her: "Great! How about a comedy club?"

Me: "Dsbrteiewocn?"

Her: "OK, how about Saturday night?"

Me: "Eiewocn?"

Her: "Great! Would seven o'clock be OK?"

Me: "Eiewo."

Her: "OK, see you then!"

To my complete and utter amazement, she graciously said, "Yes." Now why would she have to go and do something like that? I was really put on the spot. How do I act with a goddess? How do I put a sentence together? What if she didn't like me? Or worse, what if she did? I was filled with fear, excitement, and the never-ending vibrations of screaming hungry kids all at the same time!

Because this date was the end-all, be-all, mother-of-all dates, I panicked! My mind and heart had gone way beyond romance. I planned everything down to the most absurd detail. In order to ease my way into dating again, as well as to make sure the date was not over the top and too romantic, I made reservations at a well-lit, not-too-fancy, comfortable restaurant. And, it was directly across the street from the comedy club. Perfect! What could possibly go wrong?!

The word pathetic might come to mind, but it was worse than that. Rule of thumb: *Single Dad Dating* is NOT like riding a bike. I changed the same clothes 235,000 times, because I didn't know what she would be wearing. I scheduled the most important night of my life with the babysitter, cued the kids, and grew a pimple on my nose.

Since my smoke-billowing 1972 Grand Torino Station Wagon was held together by coat hangers and duct tape, and filled with sand, broken cookies, and leftover Christmas candy, my babysitter offered to let me use her car. Awesome! What a relief! "You're the greatest!" I exclaimed.

The night before my date with the most beautiful girl I'd ever met—not to mention, the first date in years—I doubled-checked, triple-checked, and checked again to make sure all was a "go" with borrowing the sitter's car the next evening. It was the same answer every time. "Absolutely! You can count on me! I'll be home all day anyway!" Great!

The countdown was on. After 23 hours and 47 minutes of hectic, sleep-deprived pacing back and forth between the living room, dining room, and all the corners of my fruit-looped mind, my MISSING-IN-ACTION, LIVE-IN babysitter f-i-n-a-l-l-y pulled into the driveway, just an hour-and-a-half before the most important event of my life was about to occur. What happened to, "I'll be home all day..."?

"I was starting to get worried!" I exclaimed as she walked toward me from her car. My anxiety-filled statement was met with a throw of her keys and a mumbling about not feeling too well. "Oh... You might want to clean the car too. I'm going to bed..." she added as she walked by at 4:17 p.m. "Huh? Not feeling well? What does that have to do with anything?" I thought to myself.

Upon my inspection of her car, it all became clear. Her "not feeling well..." apparently meant throwing up on the steering wheel, windshield, dashboard, driver's seat, ceiling, floors, down both sides of the driver's door, and window! There was half-dried vomit in every nook-n-cranny from the front bumper to the tail lights!

After navigating 22 trips through the car wash, emptying a 50-gallon drum of Pine-Sol onto the driver's seat, and spraying enough air freshener into the car to cure cancer, I made it home just in the nick of time for a very quick pre-date shower. I raced through my checklist:

- Hair? Check!
- Teeth? Check!
- Cologne? Check!
- Clean underwear? Check!
- Pimple? Check!

I felt like I was forgetting something. So I woke the babysitter up and asked for her checklist.

- Shoes? Check!
- Socks? Check!
- Coat? Check!

- Tickets? Check!
- Gas? Check!
- Pimple? Check!

Okay! It's show time! I said good night to the babysitter and kids, and away I went!

I had no idea my neurotic, scrambled-egg mind could fill the car with so many vacillating disputatious verbosities all at the same time. Before I could even get to the end of my driveway, exactly half of the voices kept demanding, "Don't be an idiot! Quit while you're ahead! You know your date's too good for you! You're a parent now and there's no way you can compete for her! So the smart thing to do is to simply turn around and go back home... Now!" The other voices retorted with, "Don't listen to those guys! Be a man! Step up to the plate! They're making too much of a deal out of this! What could possibly go wrong?! It's just a date at a comedy club! Go and have fun!" Ah... Yeah...

Can you say, "Insane"? Quite impressive, actually. There was a full-fledged, psychotic war going on in my car. Even the passersby were placing bets on who they thought would win.

The fact that I was pulling up into my To-Die-For-True-Love's driveway didn't stop this Parliamentary-style debate either. Even while I was walking up to her door, the voices kept yelling, "You fool!" "He's not a fool!" "Yes he is!" "No he's not!" "He is too!" "Will you guys shut up, for God's sake! I gotta get this together!" "Idiot!" "He's not an idiot!" "He is too!" After regaining whatever composure I could find (*none*), I walked up to the front door and knocked.

As I was yelling at the voices to shut up, the door instantly opened with a very excited and cheerful, "Hi! Let me get my purse! I'll be right back!" Wow! The voices and I were stunned! This slammed me/us directly into a slow motion euphoric haze. She was more than beautiful. She was my SOULMATE. All I could think was, "Will you marry me? I'll do anything! I'll take care of you! I'll never leave you! I'll do your dishes! Please marry me!"

During the hour-long drive to the restaurant, I was a completely tongue-twisted, mentally-decapitated, basket case of a dad who hadn't been on a date in years. I don't remember what we discussed. I just prayed my pimple wouldn't have twins.

However, about two miles from the restaurant, the car started to experience ATS (*Anxiety Transfer Syndrome*). In other words, it was becoming me. The banging and clanging of mental rubble that was going on in my head had somehow "transferred" into the car's engine. A strange knock started to come from the motor. It got louder and louder and was NOT going away! A half a mile

from the restaurant, the knocking turned into a convulsing, hic-cupping rodeo escapade, causing the car to kick and buck and jerk its way across every city intersection we entered.

For the next three straight blocks pedestrians leaped, hopped, and jumped out of our way like frantic sand fleas. A hint of smoke started to seep up through the hood. The bucking got so bad that one second we'd see the stars in the sky, and then the next sec-ond, we'd see the street. Stars! Street! Stars! Street! Stars! Street! Stars! Street! My date and I looked like a couple of life-sized bob-ble heads! I ended up with a whiplash!

Guessing at the celestial constellations strobing above us, I navi-gated our bucking capsule through city streets, alleys, and sidewalks just in time to bounce into the restaurant parking lot for our well-lit, not-too-fancy, dinner reservations. Wow! We made it! Thank God!

After reassuring my Drop-Dead-Gorgeous-Too-Good-To-Be-True-Can't-Live-Without date that I had everything "under con-trol" and that the car just needed to "cool down a bit," my right eye started to twitch. "Really? Now what? For God's sake! What?!" As the twitching increased, pictures of my original checklist rifled throughout my spaghetti & meatball mind. I became engulfed by the feeling that I had forgotten something. "What?!" WHAT?!

As we were getting out of the bronco-bucking car, I reached into my jacket for my wallet. And, well, what do you know? To my stark-raving-crazy-insane-panic-attack HORROR, I had apparently left my wallet at home! "Wait. What? Really?! No! What?! Huh? Wait! My Wallet?! What?! No! Really?! Wait?! What?! There Once Was a Girl from Nantucket! WHAT??!!! Really?!!! NO !^#!%* WAY!! Really?! MY !^#!%* WALLET!!! Really?! STUPID!! STUPID!! STUUUUPID!! Really?! REALLY?!!!"

Well obviously, the only possible solution for me at this point–
was to simply jump out of my quivering body and run across
the street to hide under a rock before my Once-In-A-Life-Time-
Chance-To-Impress date gets out of the car!

How? Am I? Going? To? Explain? THIS?!!!

I have NO !^#!%* money!!! The car is in complete and utter
!^#!%* MUTINY! And is STILL NOT DONE DYING YET!! What am
I going to !^#!%* DO?!!!

"Think fast, moron!" What to do? What to do? What to do?
Oh no!! Oh No!! She just shut her door and is walking toward the
restaurant!! Argh!! What am I going to do?!!!

I had no choice. I had to cough up and spit out my newly discovered realization–and then prepare to escort my Once-In-A-
Lifetime-Chance-To-Impress date to the nearest bus stop to look
at bus schedules. To my absolute astonishment however, my date
bestowed upon me a beatific smile, and, with the elegance and
forgiveness only known to Mother Teresa said, "That's okay. I really enjoy your company. We can go pick up your wallet and then
go to my place to get my car if you like." TILT!

Mortifying thoughts of unworthiness continued to implode
throughout every cell of my being as I also realized I had forgotten to open the door for her, but, did manage to unlock her door
from my side as I groveled myself back into the driver's seat.

We began our bronco-busting hour-long journey back home.
No matter how much confidence I attempted, my Beautiful-To-
Die-For date had no choice but to periodically ask if I thought the
car was going to make it back okay. Even though *all* of the voices in my head had unanimously regressed to childhood rants of
wanting to go home and crawl under a blanket forever and ever, I

still gave her encouraging affirmations indicating that all was well. And to everyone's amazement, we did f-i-n-a-l-l-y make it!

After picking up my wallet *and* switching cars, we headed back toward town in her car to continue on our wonderful date/adventure.

As you might imagine, the date wasn't going quite as I'd hoped. My social veneer had been thoroughly stripped off of me like I'd been skinned alive. All of my actions and comments were governed solely and completely by pure unadulterated mortification. Any chance at salvaging this "date"–let alone any chance for a romance–was, for me, gone. Kiss another dream goodbye. If I had a peanut butter sandwich, I could have at least done myself in...

We were so late getting back to the restaurant that we lost our dinner reservations and went straight to the comedy club. After standing in line for what seemed like two years, we were ushered to a seat in the bar to wait for the show's doors to open. Since we were two hours too late for our dinner, my beautiful date asked me if I was hungry. The cup of clam chowder she had seven hours earlier for lunch in anticipation of our dinner plans apparently wasn't enough to hold her through the evening.

Even though 99.17% of my life was fixated on figuring out where the kids' next meal would be coming from, did I pick up on her clue? No, of course not. It hadn't been originated by four kids blatantly screaming, "I'm hungry! I'm hungry! I'm hungry! I'm hungry!" Instead, it was politely hinted at by an intelligent, beautiful goddess speaking in adult human language. So, like a complete and utter clueless boob, I said, "No. I'm not hungry..." and pompously proceeded to express my dislike for the neon black lights glowing and pulsating above our heads.

Could I stop there? Nope! Absolutely not! I was on a roll! Being the captive audience she was, my beautiful date witnessed, with morbid curiosity, my desperate attempt to get things back on track with even more insipid and boastful digressions. No matter what I said or did, the tedious and pontificating ramblings kept cascading and plummeting out of my mouth like water going over Niagara Falls.

I was a mess and I was starving my date. The headlines read: "Man on first date starves woman and finishes her off with deranged and tedious rants." (Now, in my defense, we had been told that we couldn't bring food into the show and that the doors were supposed to have opened "any minute." Or, something like that.)

After watching a smorgasbord of sizzling, mouth-watering appetizers parade past our table for a half-an-hour, it was f-i-n-a-l-l-y time for the real comedy show to begin. We were corralled to our seats, which happened to be in the front row. Before I could excuse myself to use the restroom, the first of three comedians jumped onto the stage searching for anyone in the front row to pick on. Oh great... I was squirming in my seat just like the kids did when they had to go potty! But there was no way I was going to get up from a front row seat during a comedy show.

So, I sat and squirmed, and squirmed, and sat. My thoughts fixated and centered on one thing only. How was I going to get to the restroom before my bladder erupts? After what seemed to be an eternity of having my legs crossed so tightly for so long they were out of blood, the show was f-i-n-a-l-l-y over.

I think the comedians were funny, but because I was chasing my bladder around the table for most of the show, I don't quite remember. However, I do remember spending the next twenty-three-and-a-half minutes relieving myself in the bathroom!

With our bladders as empty as our stomachs, we made it back to my Once-In-A-Lifetime-Chance-To-Impress date's car. Filling the hour-long drive back home with more of my feeble attempts to shut the hell up, my date finally pulled over at my house and left me with a very polite and understanding, "Thank you. I had a nice time."

Knowing my chance for another date with this goddess would be so far in the future there would be daily shuttle flights to the moon by then, I waved goodbye to the girl of my dreams and watched her drive away. Defeated, I slithered into the house, sat down on the couch, and slid back into my reality. Looking at the freshly stacked parental resignation letters, and conversing with my confidante, the dog, it was time for me to realize my Romeo moves were over and it was back to parenting I go. Yippee!

The point to this chapter is, it's sometimes difficult to stray away from being a parent. No matter how much your mind tricks you into thinking you CAN "have a life," the reality is that your familial obligations and responsibilities will pull you back into *The Parenting Game!* So, suck it up butter cup! There are bills to pay! Ah, and, oh yeah, laundry to do, too.

"There is no greater wonder than the way the face and character of a woman fit so perfectly in a man's mind, and stay there, and he could never tell you why. It just seems it was the thing he most wanted."

ROBERT LOUIS STEVENSON

18

THERE'S A HOLE IN YOUR POCKET

Although my kids were ready to, and for heaven's sake I was absolutely planning on it, they didn't exactly move out to live on their own at the ripe old age of five. Wow! Sure didn't see that one coming!

This little setback will cost you a LOT more time, more worry, more hair, and lots and lots more money than you could ever possibly imagine! So much money it hasn't even been printed yet! You're on at least an 18-year financial plan—per child—which turns into an ongoing lifetime fiscal commitment.

This chapter is devoted to laying out some of the estimated costs of rearing children. It by no means covers all of the expenditures, but demonstrates some of the costs involved.

By personal observation, the manufacturers of children's paraphernalia have developed a very accurate and detailed pricing formula. It goes like this:

"All product costs specifically vary depending upon the de-mographic/psychographic phenomena of those respond-

ing to the consumer triggers implanted in them by the advertising formulas developed by the test marketing's projected figures between the years 1925 and 2017. These figures were calculated, tabulated, and then made available to the Marketing Department by the Research Department following extensive short surveys given to the individual team member's target market's uncle's nephew from the time he was two months old until he was five years of age."

Keeping that in mind, when the kids are infants, you'll want to feed them the old-fashioned natural way, by bottle. This is the normal way babies eat, and, at the time of this writing, it costs about $50 per month for regular cow's milk. Piece of cake. Right? Not so! Apparently, cow's milk turns into moldy cottage cheese when it's left in a plastic baby bottle and sits out in the sun too long! If your infant doesn't like the taste of moldy plastic cottage cheese, you'll naturally start using the more costly powered formulas.

As long as you don't maintain the clumsy habit of dumping the can of powder formula all over your kitchen, living room, and dog before each and every confounded feeding (because you haven't slept since the kid was born), those cans of formula can cost about $100—per child—per month. This is roughly double the cost of convenient cow's milk!

The spiraling out-of-control costs don't stop there. Every baby is different. You learn this tiny-but-major fact on the day they are born. Some infants will enjoy the lactose-free, sucrose-free, hypo allergenic, iron-fortified hydrolysis formulas with medium chain triglycerides. The average cost for the gourmet formula connoisseur is about $150 a month—three times the amount of the good ol' cow juice!

There are certain infants who have a digestive problem which can cause them to not only reject cow's milk, but all normal formulas as well—even the formulas in the $150-per-month range. The only option left is a prescribed formula. This very specialized formula can run you about $275 per month and has the aroma and taste of dried caterpillars soaked in ripened yeast. It is beyond awful! But the kid will drink it!

Most infants are bottle-fed for about six months before you'll want to feed them to the lions... Er, I mean feed them cereal in conjunction with their bottles. Once they get to that stage, you can gleefully step into the next phase of your five-year plan: throw a box of cereal and some milk at the kitchen table and run the other way! Taking their basic need of food into account, you can figure on spending approximately $1,800 to feed each child in the first year alone!

Don't forget about the laws of biology and physics. Their bodies keep growing, which requires more food. More food makes their bodies grow more, requiring even more food. Due to your increasing number of growing children, your expenses double, triple, and then quadruple—continuing on a never-ending upward spiral!

This may or may not sound all that bad, at first. However, you will notice a peculiar phenomenon that occurs when you feed babies. It usually necessitates the purchasing of—you guessed it—diapers. And, the more they eat, the more diapers they need. As *Super Parent Accountant*, you have to figure out the most economical way to diaper your children.

In the first year alone, you can count on changing at least 4,000+ diapers *(Yes! You read that right!)*, with a quarter of the changes by Braille because they will be done in the middle of the night. Diapers are like children—they grow in size. As the size changes, so does the price: upward and upward. It does appear there's a hole in your budget.

Diapers are necessary from birth to the training pants stage, which can last two-and-a-half years. The most convenient and popular path for you to take is to use disposable diapers. During this time, there are about six sizes from which to choose. At the newborn stage, the average number of diaper changes is between 12-16 times per day. At the training pants stage, the average is 6-8 changes per day. At the time of this writing, a cost of about $0.36 per change, adds up to an astounding expenditure of roughly $3,213.35 worth of disposable diapers—per child—during this two-and-a-half year period.

Cloth diapers are another option. Many cloth diaper providers offer package discounts that claim to save you money. There are different types of cloth diapers and relative costs. To help lessen the exposure to chemical toxins, your little prince or princess may sometimes desire diapers made from hemp, organic cotton, or a variety of designer brands.

In any event, it won't take long for you to notice a peculiar fact: cloth diapers need to be washed. Based on 3.436 washes per week, with energy costs of approximately $0.07928 per kilowatt of electricity for the electric water heater, or $0.5763 per therm for the gas water heater, you'll spend about $429.70 per year in energy and water costs during the time you use cloth diapers for your little ones.

As *Super Parent Protector and Provider*, you make sure each load of diapers is washed on the hot/cold cycle—and then, budgeting in "air-drying-for-softness" during summer, the total cost for two-and-a-half years of clean cloth diapers, including deter-gent, ranges from $1,250 to $1,950. Zowee! This doesn't even in-clude the cost of the diapers—or the replacement diapers!

There is also the option of using a baby diaper service with average costs starting at about $90 per month. This means no more piles of smelly diapers with which to greet your guests. Also, there's no more rinsing and washing baby's poop off of your Sunday's best. They do all of the dirty work for you. Along with specials, discounts, gift certificates, and other benefits including home, office, or day-care delivery, this route really isn't too bad. Per child, it works out to an average grand total of at least $2,700 for the two-and-a-half years.

Whether or not you choose not to wash the diapers yourself, it's always time to wash clothes of all kinds. In other words, it's constant laundry! Usually you're so distracted while trying to get the laundry started, you forget to put the clothes in the washer. This, of course, leaves you with a nice, fresh, clean load of soapy air when the cycle is complete. If you do manage to successfully get the clothes through the wash cycle, you're theoretically ready to move them over to the dryer—that is, if the kids haven't filled the dryer full of syrup and rocks—again.

Basic rule: clothes need time to dry. Timing is everything when drying clothes. In your normal haphazard daily rush, you'll only al-low 30-60 seconds for drying before having to slip on semi-wet clothes for a job interview or something. This is the usual pattern: It's dryer time! You race to the washer to be greeted by a load of cold, waterlogged, soggy clothes, because one of your kids had decided to open the lid right after you got it started. Tossing dripping wet clothes into the dryer, you pop into the shower for the luxury of 30 seconds of alone time—wash, shampoo, and rinse. Dressing takes a particular skill, because everything is still semi-wet. Hoping no one will notice, you head to your job interview. You are out to impress!

Do you include washing the empty loads in your budget? Or clothes that need five hours to dry because they were sopping wet? Nope! There's never any mention of these types of unanticipated expenses in the Parent's Manual, which are the norm and not the exception. In simple, down-to-earth terms, there's a hole in your pocket—and it's leaking money.

At some point, you might want to budget in items such as nursery monitors. I found these to be completely unnecessary, by the way. When my kids were infants, I could hear them scream and cry no matter how far I tried to get away! Same with two-way communication devices. What exactly are you supposed to say to a screaming, wet, and hungry infant at 2 a.m.? "Have your people call my people, we'll do lunch"?

If you think the costs for food and diapers will set you back a few bucks, don't forget there are other paraphernalia included when raising children: safety gates, strollers, highchairs, cribs, walkers, day cradles, swings, backpack kiddy seats, rocking horses, tricycles, starter bikes, training wheels, bikes, more bikes, bike parts, wagons, swing sets, swimming pools, toy boxes, lost shoes, haircuts, car seats, computers, computer games, etc. etc. etc.

This is not to mention other unexpected expenses—anything from repairing a family heirloom that has been smashed to smithereens, to replacing broken windows, to repainting your neighbor's fence... All in all, these expenses can send you into a never-ending financial tailspin!

Conservatively, you'll spend an estimated grand total average of about $20,000 per child. This is just for the first five years of their lives—AND, you haven't even started saving for college yet! That hole in your pocket is now growing toward the size of the National Debt! But wait, there's more!

Another hole in your pocket might be your car...

> "D'you call life a bad job? Never! We've had our ups and downs, we've had our struggles, we've always been poor, but it's been worth it, ay, worth it a hundred times I say when I look round at my children."
>
> W. SOMERSET MAUGHAM

19

CARS

Cars are a necessity when you have kids. And, just like kids, you have to nurture and pamper them. Cars are wonderful when acting properly, but quite indescribable when not. And somewhere in between, there are the days you just get by.

If you want to learn how to roll the window up or down, or how to turn on the radio, you can always refer to the Owner's Manual. However, you are going to learn the rest of your *DIY (Do-It-Yourself) Mechanic* experience by trial and error.

Ah, the errors... Here are a couple of my personal experiences.

For example, when changing a starter, it is highly recommended to disconnect the battery cable from it first. After all, while lying under the car, there's not much room between the face and the starter. Forgetting that little tidbit only happened to me once. As the socket wrench sparked out of my hand from accidentally touching the car frame, while at the same time touching the live battery cable, my face bounced onto the cold steel of the frame, which resulted in giving me a shiner that made me look as though I had just gone 10 rounds with Mike Tyson.

When I climbed out from under the car to find my three-year-old under the hood busily poking around with a screwdriver, I realized working on cars might be a great opportunity for *Mechanic Super Dad* to teach the kids the first lesson in auto mechanics, *How To Take Care of Tools!* I quickly taught them to always put the tools back into the toolbox rather than leaving them stuck in the grass to be run over and chewed up by the lawn mower. Needless to say, the lawn mower was usually on the losing end of those battles.

While these intermittent electrical problems were extremely frustrating, in my defense, I had always figured out problems with guitars and guitar systems pretty well. This was particularly pertinent when my three-year-old felt compelled to use my guitar amp as his piggy bank, dropping change into the top of the amplifier without me knowing. Naturally, a penny became lodged between the power and speaker wires, causing the $500 (each) speakers to combust into flames when I turned on the amp. Why the manufacturer put these two wires so close together in the first place was beyond me, but at least, I could figure out what was wrong.

One day I left the coffee shop armed with my trusty *Triple-Quad-Grande-Something-or-Other-Latte*, and was heading out to take my Philosophy of Religion final. I hopped into my 1972 Grand Torino Station Wagon, overflowing with car seats and cookies, and turned the key in the ignition. Nothing. Only silence. As I tried to start the car several more times, my special prayer morphed into, *"God save me! Oh God. Please save me from having to redo the Philosophy of Religion Class!"*

Because of the absolute silence when I turned the key, my first couple of guesses were along the lines of, either the battery was completely dead, or the alternator hadn't charged it properly.

A passerby asked me if I needed a jump. Switching to my best "needing a friend" personality, I exclaimed, "Yes! God bless you! You are a life saver! I owe you beyond belief! I'll do your dishes!"

There was hope. I knew I would be a little late for my final, but I could definitely finish in time! We hooked up the jumper cables, he revved up his engine, and I jumped into the car and turned the key. Ah, the not-so-sweet sound of silence. I tried again and again. Nothing. Not a sound. "This can't be happening!" I kept repeating, as the "life saver" packed up his cables and drove away.

And then I knew. The car was in on the conspiracy—with my parents, the kids, and the wannabe-show-dog (who I'd thought was my friend and confidant). The car sighed and settled in for a nap while I jogged to not one, but two auto part stores to find new battery cables. Even the sales clerks agreed replacing the battery cables was the logical solution for the problem.

Since my mechanical task was becoming more and more time sensitive, my attempts at suppressing my anxiety were slowly deteriorating. So, as quickly as possible, I crawled under the car to change the cables to have access to the starter. Reconnecting everything, I hopped back into the car and turned the ignition. Not a sound. My positive attitude changed to pure, unadulterated, frantic panic. I jumped out and cleaned off the battery poles and clamps. I made sure the fan belt to the alternator was tight. No change.

Next, I took out the starter and hauled it to the auto parts store to have it checked. Naturally, as it turned out, there was nothing wrong with it at all. This wasn't surprising. Deflated and dejected, I walked back to my car, and reinstalled the starter. I went through my mental checklist, and decided it was either the alternator, or the car just wanted some pampering. Begging on bended knee, I pleaded with the car, promised it super-duper racing quality oil, and offered a car-wash-a-week. Nothing.

I hoped my Philosophy of Religion Professor Sigmund Whampt De Whumpf would allow me a makeup test. Yeah, right. This wasn't high school.

A man in the parking lot noticed my desperate pleas, and came to offer his assistance. He was a Godsend: a mechanic for 30 years! Forget the final. That ship sailed. Now, I had to get the car started to be home in time for the kids when they got home from school.

With his voltage meter, he checked the electrical parts of the car. After a minute or so, he looked up with a puzzled look on his face. He quietly returned to putting the electrodes on different parts of the battery and engine.

Godsend: "I'll be darned."

Me: "What?"

Godsend: "If I didn't see this with my own eyes, I'd never believe it."

Me: "What?"

Godsend: "Your car has switched polarities."

Me: "Huh?"

Godsend: "Your car has switched polarities."

Me: "What do I do?"

Godsend: "I've been a mechanic for 30 years and I've never seen this."

Me: "What do I do?"

Godsend: "I don't know. Sorry I couldn't be of more assistance."

He wrapped up his meter, and no matter how much begging

and pleading I did, he left. I walked back to the first auto parts store. By now, we were on a first-name basis...

Me: "A mechanic used a meter and discovered that the car had switched polarities."

John: "That's impossible."

Me: "But I saw it."

John: "I don't know what you saw, but what you're describing is impossible. Hey Frank, I got a good one for you."

Frank: "Yeah?"

John: "Izzy's back. He says that a mechanic used a meter and discovered that the car had switched polarities."

Both chuckled.

Me: "What do I do?"

John: "I don't know. Sorry I couldn't be of more assistance."

I went to the other auto parts store and it went like this:

Me: "A mechanic used a meter and discovered that the car had switched polarities."

George: "That's impossible."

Me: "But I saw it."

George: "I don't know what you saw, but what you're describing is impossible. Hey Sam, I got a good one for you."

Sam: "Yeah?"

George: "Izzy's back. He says that a mechanic used a meter and discovered that the car had switched polarities."

Both chuckled.

Me: "What do I do?"

George: "I don't know. Sorry I couldn't be of more assistance."

I went back to the car, distraught, empty-handed, and without any solutions. It was six hours later and I just barely had time to start walking home to be there when the kids got out of school. In utter dismay, I closed the hood, got into the car, and with a very humble and sincere, "Please, God." I gave it one last try. And, what do you know—it started!

After a tremendous amount of calculations and hard work, I discovered why my 1972 Grand Torino Station Wagon had, in fact, switched polarities. It was very simple. The car was BIPOLAR! And it HATED me.

Car problems nearly nickel and dimed me into complete financial ruin. This was an important factor since I was trying to keep food on the table for my kids. And, just like the kids, the car could sniffle out any extra money I had, using its cunning wiles to suck every penny out of my pocket. To help illustrate this even further:

Another electrical problem happened right in the middle of a Northwest Torrential 32.5° November Rain—a perfect cue for the car to know precisely when to break down. Timing was everything, and the car was an expert.

On this freezing cold winter evening, I had raced to my favorite pawn shop to release my precious music equipment for the sum of $375. After loading the gear into the car, and waving goodbye to the owner, I was ready to race to the grocery store, pick up dinner, and head home before it snowed!

Yay? Nope. NOT YAY. No matter how many times I turned the key, the car just would not start. Not even a peep. The next thing I knew, I was ravaging through all my music gear to get down to my tools!

Determined to get home in time for dinner, I dove under the car to check out the starter. With the ridiculous downpour, my body became some sort of a downtown "gutter-dam," blocking tidal waves of oil-soaked cigarette butts, candy wrappers, and God-knows-what-else swelling up over my chest, face, and streaming long hair. The freezing rain was coming down so hard it was all I could do to gasp up for air and not get sucked under! This river had rapids and currents so magnificent, bears were trying to catch the salmon as they flew out of the water to spawn!

Following a few more spurts of vulgarities and hurling wrenches at the car, I finally got the starter to come loose. Now, completely drenched and swollen from the cold, waterlogged clothes, I started on my way to the nearest auto parts store.

Did the auto parts store just around the corner have a starter that fit my car? Nope. Of course not! The cashier person told me the next closest auto parts store was 22 blocks across town. With my 16.5-pound starter in hand, I began my Northwest Trek to that store. Upon arrival and inspection of my starter, I was assured the new starter would fit my car. I paid them the $78, and set off on the 22-block hike back to my car. Well wouldn't you know it? The new starter didn't quite fit and no matter how many times I screamed and kicked the car, it just wouldn't start!

I figured it had to be the battery so I called a taxi for a $25 jump. An hour later, the cab arrived, and we discovered the attempt to jump the car didn't work either. For an additional $37.50, the cab driver would take me home. But first, I dragged my music equipment back into the pawnshop—through the revolving door they had put in just for me—to get a new loan to fix my car. Running cost so far: $140.50. (Granted, this doesn't sound like much, but when you don't have it—YOU DON'T HAVE IT!)

Once home, I was greeted with the usual task of finding two missing homework assignments and inventing some sort of dinner out of peanut butter & macaroni. On top of this, I had to tolerate snide comments from my much-needed, little-miss-know-it-all-girly babysitter, who kept insisting the problem wasn't the starter or battery; it was the alternator. How would she know? She was just a girl!

Next, I phoned my lead singer and pleaded with him to help me tow my station wagon home. Despite his protests and silly little excuses like, "Your car is way too big for my Mazda B210 to tow!" and, "I don't have the gas to drive you all over the place!" he reluctantly agreed. Of course, I promised to pay him $50 for his trouble. Running cost now: $190.50.

In the morning, he picked me up and we rented a tow bar for the day. This only cost $120. After jerry-rigging a too-big-for-his-car tow bar between the two cars and reassuring him all would be okay, we were off. Yikes! Running cost now: $310.50.

We hadn't gone very far when the 1972 Grand Torino Station Wagon gracefully swung up alongside us to face the opposite direction. Watching the station wagon jackknife both vehicles across two lanes in slow-motion was somewhat surreal—but oddly, also quite normal—to me.

While listening to my singer scream five octaves worth of obscenities about having no license, no insurance, and a newly acquired bent fender, a truck driver (who was now stuck behind us) and I lifted the twisted Mazda, turned it (and the still-screaming singer) in the appropriate direction, and pushed my car off the road. This was just in time to wave a polite hello to a city's worth of not-so-happy motorists who had been waiting for the past 22 minutes to get around us.

We then raced back to my house to call a tow truck to pick up my car. Next, we played the game, *Can We Get Back to My Car in Time to Divert a Ticket from the State Patrol and Having My Car Impounded?* Won! The tow home cost me $150. Running cost was now up to $460.50.

Between the barrages of, "I'm telling you, it's the alternator!" coming from little-miss-know-it-all-girly babysitter, and helping my 10-year-old put the chain back on his younger brother's bike (because he had used it to tie the other brother to a tree), I managed to remove the new 462-pound starter from the car. During 30 minutes of vicious silence, my singer drove the starter and me to the auto parts store for a much-needed replacement, as well as an explanation of why it didn't fit.

The clerk I saw the day before wasn't there, but another one was more than willing to help me. He said, "Oh, well that's your problem right there..."—as if I was a complete idiot. "It's the wrong size! See? See right there?" He pointed to the starter shaft. "Here, let's give you this one..." he continued with a belittling smile and a wave goodbye.

Despite 30 minutes of, "I told you so!" from the lead singer, 300 bouts of, "I'm hungry!" from the kids, and another round of, "I'm telling you, it's the alternator!" from my little-miss-know-it-all-girly babysitter, I put the new starter in the car. I climbed in, cranked the key, and guess what? Nothing!

With the crazed and hectic precision of a bat on fire, and froth seething from my nostrils, I madly followed all of the wires from the starter, to the moon, and back again. Nothing! It all *looked* good. However, while leaning in for a closer look—just when little-miss-know-it-all-girly babysitter came out to remind me we needed more food—I rested my hand on the alternator for a little more balance. The alternator swung down off the mount. "Well I'll be..." I thought to myself.

"Yeah, see! Right there! If you tighten that bolt back up, the car will start!" exclaimed the little-miss-know-it-all-girly babysitter sarcastically, as she rolled her eyes. "Oh ya, and by the way, you still owe me $35 for working late yesterday and this morning!"

And, well, what do you know? It started. The grand total for a loose bolt was $460.50. Of course, this didn't include the $375 needed to get my equipment out of hock (again) and $35 to pay the little-miss-know-it-all-girly babysitter!

Besides regular maintenance, electrical problems weren't the only things that went wrong with the car. Water pumps went out, tires blew, and axles fell off. Hoods flew open, the gas tank leaked, and radiators blew up. And then there was the time I was in the waiting room during a routine ER visit, when the car caught fire because the muffler was coat-hangered too close to the floorboard. The car wanted my attention—and got it! I could only guess what was going to happen next. It was like having another kid.

Car problems never happen at a convenient time or place. There's nothing like having to face the challenges of being out in the middle of nowhere, 100 miles away from home, broken down late on a Sunday night with a car full of tired, wet, and hungry kids. How does it get any better than this?

"Macho does not prove mucho."

ZSA ZSA GABOR

20

AT THE END OF THE DAY

From the second your kids are born, they are yours—unconditionally. You have them and they have you. *All* of you. The parent-child bond has been fused before your child even takes his or her first breath of fresh air. And with that first wail, the union is solidified. You are their *Protector, Defender, Guide, Teacher, Willing Subject, Obedient Supplicant,* and *Champion.* You are all of these things to them—forever.

Despite the countless wrong decisions, doubts, and what-ifs that pour through your mind, at the end of each day, your children will always allow you as many second chances as you will ever need. By virtue of their innocent and unconditional love, they will show you by example that people can, in fact, have such attributes as tolerance, open-mindedness, and patience—especially patience. Remember patience? **The bearing of provocation, annoyance, and pain without complaint or irritation or loss of temper.** Well, deep down inside, *they* have it. And it's all for you.

Yup. You will learn a lot from your kids. No matter what, you can be certain they will be there to pick you up, brush you off, and scoot you back in the right direction again. They know just how and when to give you understanding, sympathy, and even tough love—right when you need it most.

Their patience and guidance continues from diaper stage, through childhood, and into the great beyond. This is when you watch them grow into young adults, climbing their own ladders of success. This is where you feel the rewards of all those years coming to life before you. Yup. This is it! This is what it's all about!

From the beginning of parenthood to your retirement from it, your goal is to watch all of your years of devotion manifest your offspring into productive, pillars of society. This is when you can finally tell yourself, "Job well done!" But until then, it's a lot of hard work to get them there. Necessity will get you through it! In the following chapter, *21 Tips for Terrific Parenting*, I share some of my own tips and suggestions to help you on your journey.

"Parents learn a lot from their children about coping with life."

MURIEL SPARK

21

21 TIPS FOR TERRIFIC PARENTING

Now, I am not a child psychologist, nor do I claim to be one on TV. However, based on my own experiences, I have put together some simple tips for pre-parents and young parents to consider.

Keep in mind, no advice can really stand up to the non-stop roller coaster of mental and emotional kaleidoscopic dichotomies parents experience on a day-to-day basis. When in doubt, punt. While some of these suggestions may seem unorthodox, they worked for me!

1. Have a sense of humor. If you don't have one, find one. Things happen. "Expect the unexpected" is the only parental blueprint there is. So suck it up, buttercup. You're in for the ride of your life!

2. Have patience. Patience is a must, and especially with a large family. There will be many instances when you are going to function with very little sleep (or none at all), and sometimes, for days on end.

3. Parents can have nervous breakdowns. Do you have what it

takes to be a fair judge, jury, and executioner during these exciting moments?

4. Can you make instant life-changing split decisions, while at the same time hunting down and changing a wet, poopy diaper before it runs across your neighbor's front yard–again?

5. Don't take parenting too personally. All parents have parental regrets on a daily basis. The "should haves, could haves, and would haves" pile up. Do not fixate on them. Learn. And move on!

6. When your child comes to you with particular requests, do you know when to say, "Yes," when to say, "No," and why?

7. Never ever go back on your word. You make a promise? Keep it!

8. If you tell your children they are grounded, never ever let it slide. Not once!

9. Build a sense of responsibility in your kids as early as possible. Help them pick a task which exemplifies positive reinforcement. This could be doing a simple chore, such as turning off their bedroom lights at night, or reminding you to buy diapers at the store. As long as they can have some decision-making authority, they will appreciate being in control of at least a small part of their environment. Plus, the sooner they learn how to do something, the easier it becomes for everyone.

10. Sincerely ask your kids for advice. You would be amazed at what they come up with.

11. If your child comes to you with an issue or problem, make sure you listen. Acknowledge it, and then ask what he or she thinks should be done about it. In a lot of cases, your child may realize how he or she could have been the one who actually created the problem in the first place.

12. Always be prepared. Have a First Aid Kit, extra diapers, bottles, snacks, toys, etc. with you at all times.

13. Make time for yourself. Nobody else will.

14. Get your kids to the starting gate as best as you can. Then, get out of their way!

15. If you find yourself on a plane with your nine-month-old baby, remember that babies do not understand how to "pop" their ears as the plane climbs or descends. They scream! One trick is to close off their nose and mouth (as if you were having them blow their nose) just before they scream. This helps the ears pop, and it only takes a nanosecond. It keeps the other passengers happy too.

16. I know I wrote about this in Chapter 2, *Beddy-Bye Time*, but I cannot emphasize this point enough: **Let a sleeping baby lie!**

17. If you have a weak stomach, get over it! Babies will poop, pee, and throw up on you at the most unexpected moments–usually when you're just heading in to a job interview!

18. Be ambidextrous. You will be changing diapers, filling bottles, answering phones, applying bandages, etc.–*all at the same time.*

19. Learn how to cook. And, teach the kids how to cook.

20. Allow the kids to explore their interests early.

21. Set a good example. Kids watch your every move.
Good luck!

ABOUT THE AUTHOR

Israel (Izzy) Rehaume was born and raised in Seattle, Washington. As a teenager, he worked at the well-known Edgewater Inn in Seattle, primarily as a garde manger, carving ice sculptures and entering culinary arts competitions. By age 19, he was an accomplished guitarist and bass player, working with several rock bands throughout the Pacific Northwest and Canada.

In the mid 1980's, Izzy acquired four sons and became the proud single parent musician he is today. After the kids were grown, Izzy's endeavors led him to pursue many different music projects with a number of musicians playing and performing in the United States and Europe. As an author and screenwriter, Izzy currently has a variety of media projects in development as well as continuing to write, compose, and produce many styles of songs and music to make available for licensing.

As for Izzy's kids, two are now professional entertainers based out of Los Angeles, one is a successful contractor in Seattle and his youngest son served his country as a United States Marine. Oh, and that lovely creature from Date Night? That is the love of his life, and now his wife.

CPSIA information can be obtained
at www.ICGtesting.com
Printed in the USA
FSOW03n0354300817
38018FS

9 781946 928085